cook's library
Wok &
Stir-Fry

cook's library

Wok &
Stir-Fry

p

This is a Parragon Book
This edition published in 2003

Parragon
Queen Street House
4 Queen Street
Bath BA1 1HE, UK

ISBN: 0-75259-442-7

Printed in China

NOTE

This book uses metric and imperial measurements. Follow the same
units of measurement throughout; do not mix metric and imperial.
All spoon measurements are level: teaspoons are assumed to be 5 ml,
and tablespoons are assumed to be 15 ml. Unless otherwise stated,
milk is assumed to be full fat, eggs and individual vegetables, such as
potatoes are medium, and pepper is freshly ground black pepper.

The times given for each recipe are an approximate guide only because
the preparation times may differ according to the techniques used by
different people and the cooking times may vary as a result of the type
of oven used. The preparation times include chilling and marinating
times, where appropriate.

Recipes using raw or very lightly cooked eggs should be
avoided by infants, the elderly, pregnant women, convalescents
and anyone suffering from an illness.

Contents

Introduction

One of the quickest, easiest and most versatile methods of cooking is to stir-fry in a wok. It takes only a few minutes to assemble the ingredients – a selection of vegetables, to which may be added meat, fish, seafood, tofu, nuts, rice or noodles. The possibilities are endless; ring the changes with different oils, seasonings and sauces, and the result is a colourful, delicious, healthy meal that is as pleasing to the eye as it is to the tastebuds.

Wok

A wok is a metal cooking implement in the shape of a shallow, curved bowl, with either one long wooden handle or two looped handles. The wok comes in a variety of sizes – one approximately 30–35-cm/12–14-inches in diameter is suitable for the average family – and, as with most kitchen equipment, it is worth investing in the best you can. Woks are made from stainless steel, copper or cast iron, and the latter is ideal as it retains heat more efficiently, especially once it has become well-seasoned.

Although it is possible to stir-fry in a frying pan, there are several good reasons to use a wok. The key to successful stir-frying is to move and toss the ingredients constantly as they cook, and this is much easier to achieve in the convex shape of a wok. The curved sides allow the heat to rise, so that the whole wok becomes hot, speeding up the cooking process; and as the food cannot become lodged in corners or edges, it is extremely easy to clean the wok after use.

Wok Seasoning and Cleaning

New woks, apart from those with a non-stick lining, must be seasoned before they are used. First wash well with hot water and cream cleanser to remove the protective coating of oil. Rinse and dry the wok and then place it over a low heat and add about 2 tablespoons of vegetable oil. Rub the oil all over the inner surface of the wok with a thick pad of kitchen paper, taking care not to burn your fingers. Heat the oil for about 10 minutes, then wipe it off with a fresh pad of kitchen paper, which will become black. Repeat this heating and wiping process until the kitchen paper remains clean; it will take quite a long time.

Once the wok has been seasoned, it should not be washed with cream cleanser or detergent. Simply wipe it out with kitchen paper, wash in hot water and dry thoroughly. If the wok is used only occasionally, it may become rusty. In this case, scour the rust off and season again.

Wok Accessories

Some woks are supplied with lids, but if not, these can be bought separately. They are dome-shaped, usually made of aluminium and are tight-fitting. A lid is necessary when the wok is used for steaming, but a dome-shaped saucepan lid will work as satisfactorily.

A metal stand is an essential safety feature when the wok is used for steaming, braising or deep-frying. It may be an open-sided frame or a perforated metal ring.

A wok scoop is a bowl-shaped spatula with a long handle. Some resemble a perforated spoon and others are made from reinforced wire mesh. The handle may be wood or metal. The scoop makes it easier to toss the ingredients during stir-frying, but a long-handled spoon is an adequate substitute. Chinese cooks also use the scoop for adding ingredients to the wok.

A trivet is used for steaming. It is placed in the base of the wok and supports the dish or plate containing the food above the water level. It may be made of wood or metal.

A wok brush of split bamboo is used for cleaning the wok.

For steaming, bamboo baskets with lids are available in a range of sizes and can be stacked one on top of another. They are designed to rest on the sloping sides of the wok above the water level.

The cleaver is a finely balanced tool that is seen in every Chinese kitchen. It is used for virtually all cutting tasks, from chopping spare ribs and halving duck to slashing fish and deveining prawns. Cleavers are available in a variety of weights and sizes and although they look unwieldy, they are precision instruments. The blade should be kept razor sharp.

Long wooden chopsticks may be used for adding ingredients to the wok, fluffing rice, separating noodles and general stirring. They are not essential, but are useful and add a feeling of authenticity. Because they have a lighter touch than a spoon or fork, they are less likely to break up or squash delicate ingredients. Chopsticks are easy to handle once you have acquired the knack. Place one chopstick in the angle between your thumb and index finger, with the lower part resting on your middle finger. Hold the other chopstick between the thumb and index finger as you would hold a pencil; this is the one you manipulate.

Regional Cookery

Although its popularity is now far more wide-ranging, wok cooking originated in Asia and the Far East, where variations of this useful implement are commonly used in the preparation of many dishes. In India, the curry derives its name from karahi, a large pan that sits over a hole in a brick or earth oven and is used for braising and frying, while in Mongolia the convex iron griddle used for barbecuing meat, especially lamb, is very similar in shape to a wok.

It was the Chinese, however, who devised stir-frying in a wok. There are regional variations in ingredients throughout this vast country, but fresh vegetables play a very important role in all Chinese cooking. This rapid and efficient method of cooking vegetables ensures that they retain their individual flavours, their vibrant colours and their crisp texture, as well as preserving their vitamin content. Poultry, lamb, beef and pork are also cooked in the wok – either stir-fried or steamed – and are combined with sauces and seasonings. Long- or short-grain rice is often added or served as an accompaniment, and noodles made from wheat, buckwheat or rice flours are also widely used.

Chinese influence has spread to its neighbouring countries. Throughout Indonesia, Japan, Thailand, Singapore and Malaysia, the wok is used over wood or charcoal for curries and rice dishes as well as stir-fries, with variations in the addition of different meat, fish, vegetables, spices and sauces.

A style of cuisine that has enjoyed a huge rise in popularity in recent years is Thai. For the people of Thailand, the preparation and eating of good food, beautifully served, is taken very seriously. The ingredients, locally grown and very fresh, are carefully chosen and skillfully balanced for texture and flavour, combining bitter, salt, sour, hot and sweet tastes.

Thai cooking lends itself perfectly to stir-frying. There are many Thai dishes that are cooked in a wok, either one-pot noodle recipes or vegetable, fish, meat and even soup dishes.

The monsoon climate and abundant rainfall in Thailand produce ideal conditions for growing rice, so it's not surprising that Thai cuisine is centred around this, the country's most important staple. Thai fragrant rice is a long-grain, fluffy white rice, delicately scented, while glutinous rice is short-grain with a high starch content, which makes it sticky when cooked. Rice flour is also used to make noodles, usually in the shape of flat ribbons or thin vermicelli.

The warm Gulf seas around Thailand, and the inland waterways, produce a wide variety of fish in abundance, and in all the coastal towns fresh seafood is sold from thatch-roofed beach kiosks – barbecued or sautéed fish with ginger, prawns with coconut milk and coriander, or steamed crab. Meat is often combined with seafood, such as prawns or crab meat.

Other essentials in Thai cooking are coconut (almost as important as rice), lime, chilli, garlic, lemon grass, root ginger and coriander, as well as seasonings, such as soy sauce, rice vinegar and Thai fish sauce. All of these ingredients are now readily available in your local supermarket.

Cooking Techniques

Although the wok can be used for steaming and deep-frying, its main use is for stir-frying. In China, where this is the most widely used method of cooking, it is called *Ch'au*, a term that describes cooking a number of ingredients, thinly sliced, in oil. As it cooks, the food is tossed and turned with bamboo chopsticks.

There are two basic types of stir-frying, known as *Pao* and *Liu*. *Pao*, or 'explosion', is a method where the food is stirred rapidly in a dry wok over the highest heat for about one minute. Foods cooked in this way are often marinated beforehand for flavour and tenderness. *Liu* is wet frying, where the foods are constantly turned until cooked. Peanut or corn oil are usually used for stir-frying. Sesame oil burns easily, but can be drizzled over the finished dish as a seasoning.

Some foods need a slightly longer cooking time than others and, for this reason, stir-frying is often done in stages. This also allows the individual ingredients to retain their distinct flavours. As they cook, the foods are removed from the wok, but they are always combined once everything is cooked, and served as a whole dish. In *Liu*, a mixture of cornflour and stock, mixed to a paste, is added to the wok at the end of cooking, together with sugar, vinegar and soy sauce, to make a delicious, almost sticky coating sauce.

There is plenty of scope for creativity when choosing ingredients, even for the simplest stir-fry. A combination of onions, carrots, peppers (green, red, yellow and orange), broccoli and mangetout will provide the basis for a colourful dish. Add beansprouts at the end of cooking and toss quickly for texture, or some canned water chestnuts, which add a delicious crunch. A few cashew nuts or almonds, some cubed tofu or chicken breast, or a handful of prawns provide protein, while adding some pre-cooked rice or noodles makes a gutsy stir-fry. A ready-made sauce – perhaps oyster or yellow bean – will finish off the dish. Ginger, garlic and chillies are wonderful for flavouring stir-fries. Chillies come in a wide variety, ranging in heat from very mild to fiery hot. Red chillies are slightly sweeter and hotter than green, and larger chillies also tend to be milder. Crushed dried chillies are useful for seasoning. The Thais favour the small red or green 'bird's-eye' chillies, which are very fiery, and their curries are also strongly flavoured with ferociously spicy hot chilli pastes.

Some of the 'kick' can be taken out of a hot chilli by removing the seeds, but this must be done carefully as they can cause a nasty reaction if contact is made with the skin. Cut fresh chillies in half, and scrape out the seeds with the point of a knife, and with dried chillies, simply cut off the end and shake out the seeds. Always remember to wash your hands after handling chillies!

How to Use This Book

Each recipe contains a wealth of useful information, including a breakdown of nutritional quantities, preparation and cooking times, and level of difficulty. All of this information is explained in detail below.

A full-colour photograph of the finished dish.

The ingredients for each recipe are listed in the order that they are used.

The nutritional information provided for each recipe is per serving or per portion. Optional ingredients, variations or serving suggestions have not been included in the calculations.

The green lentils used in this recipe require soaking but it's worth the time for the flavour. If time is short, use red split lentils that don't need soaking.

WOK & STIRFRY

17

Green Lentil Pan-fry

SERVES 4

150 g/5½ oz dried green lentils
4 tbsp butter or vegetarian margarine
2 garlic cloves, crushed
2 tbsp olive oil
1 tbsp cider vinegar
1 red onion, cut into 8 pieces
50 g/1¾ oz baby corn cobs, halved lengthways
1 yellow pepper, deseeded and cut into strips
1 red pepper, deseeded and cut into strips
50 g/1¾ oz green beans, halved
125 ml/4 fl oz vegetable stock
2 tbsp honey
salt and pepper
crusty bread, to serve

1 Soak the lentils in a large saucepan of cold water for 25 minutes. Bring to the boil, reduce the heat and simmer for 20 minutes. Drain thoroughly.

2 Add 1 tablespoon of the butter, 1 garlic clove, 1 tablespoon of oil and the vinegar to the lentils and mix well.

3 Add the remaining butter and oil to a preheated wok or large, heavy-based frying pan and when hot add the remaining garlic, the onion, corn cobs, peppers and green beans and stir-fry for 3–4 minutes.

4 Add the vegetable stock and bring to the boil. Cook the mixture for about 10 minutes, or until the liquid has evaporated.

5 Add the honey and season with salt and pepper to taste. Stir in the lentil mixture and cook for 1 minute to heat through. Spoon on to warmed serving plates and serve with crusty bread.

NUTRITION
Calories 490; Sugars 12 g; Protein 26 g; Carbohydrates 61 g; Fat 18 g; Saturates 8 g

easy
30 mins
45 mins

COOK'S TIP
This stir-fry is very versatile – you can use a mixture of any of your favourite vegetables, if you prefer, such as courgettes, carrots and mangetout.

The method is clearly explained with step-by-step instructions that are easy to follow.

Cook's tips provide useful information regarding ingredients or cooking techniques.

The number of stars represents the difficulty of each recipe, ranging from very easy (1 star) to challenging (4 stars).

This amount of time represents the preparation of ingredients, including cooling, chilling and soaking times.

This represents the cooking time.

Soups *and* Starters

Soup is indispensable at Asian tables, especially in China, Japan, Korea and South-East Asia. It is generally eaten part way through a main meal to clear the palate for further dishes. There are many different types of delicious soups, both thick and thin and, of course, the clear soups that are often served with wontons or dumplings in them. Starters or snacks are drier foods in general; the spring roll is a well-known Chinese snack and these come in many variations and shapes across the Far East. Other delights are wrapped in pastry, bread and rice paper or are skewered for ease of eating; vegetables, fish and meat are also deep-fried for a crispy coating. These dishes are served as starters in Westernised restaurants to animate the tastebuds ready for the main course.

Hot and sour soups are found across South-East Asia in different forms. Reduce the number of chillies added, if you prefer a milder dish.

Hot *and* Sour Mushroom Soup

SERVES 4

2 tbsp tamarind paste
4 fresh red chillies, chopped very finely
2 garlic cloves, crushed
2 tsp finely chopped fresh root ginger
4 tbsp fish sauce
2 tbsp palm sugar or caster sugar
8 lime leaves, torn roughly
1.25 litres/2 pints vegetable stock
100 g/3½ oz carrots, sliced thinly
225 g/8 oz button mushrooms, halved
350 g/12 oz white cabbage, shredded
100 g/3½ oz fine green beans, halved
3 tbsp roughly chopped fresh coriander
100 g/3½ oz cherry tomatoes, halved

1 Place the tamarind paste, red chillies, garlic, ginger, fish sauce, palm sugar, lime leaves and vegetable stock in a large preheated wok or large, heavy-based saucepan. Bring the mixture to the boil, stirring occasionally.

2 Reduce the heat and add the carrots, mushrooms, white cabbage and green beans. Leave the soup to simmer, uncovered, for about 10 minutes, or until the vegetables are tender, but not soft.

3 Stir the fresh coriander and cherry tomatoes into the mixture in the wok and heat through for another 5 minutes.

4 Transfer the soup to a warm soup tureen or individual serving bowls and serve immediately.

NUTRITION
Calories *87*; Sugars *7 g*; Protein *4 g*;
Carbohydrate *8 g*; Fat *5 g*; Saturates *1 g*

easy

10 mins

20 mins

🍲 **COOK'S TIP**

Tamarind is the dried fruit of the tamarind tree. Sold as a pulp or paste, it is used to give a special sweet and sour flavour to Oriental dishes.

Crab and sweetcorn are classic ingredients in Chinese cooking. Here, egg noodles are added for a filling dish.

Crab *and* Sweetcorn Soup

1 Heat the sunflower oil in a preheated wok or large, heavy-based saucepan.

2 Add the Chinese five-spice powder, carrots, sweetcorn, peas, spring onions and chilli to the wok and cook for about 5 minutes, stirring constantly.

3 Add the crab meat to the wok and stir-fry the mixture for 1 minute, distributing the crab evenly.

4 Roughly break up the egg noodles and add to the wok.

5 Pour the fish stock and soy sauce into the wok and bring to the boil.

6 Cover the wok or frying pan and leave the soup to simmer for 5 minutes.

7 Stir once more, then transfer the soup to a warm soup tureen or individual serving bowls and serve immediately.

SERVES 4

1 tbsp sunflower oil
1 tsp Chinese five-spice powder
225 g/8 oz carrots, cut into sticks
150 g/5½ oz canned or frozen sweetcorn
75 g/2¾ oz frozen peas
6 spring onions, trimmed and sliced
1 fresh red chilli, deseeded and very
    sliced thinly
400 g/14 oz canned white crab meat
175 g/6 oz egg noodles
1.7 litres/3 pints fish stock
3 tbsp soy sauce

NUTRITION
Calories 324; Sugars *6 g*; Protein *27 g*;
Carbohydrate *39 g*; Fat *8 g*; Saturates *2 g*

⭐⭐   easy
🕐   5 mins
🕐   20 mins

👨‍🍳 **COOK'S TIP**

Chinese five-spice powder is a mixture of star anise, fennel, cloves, cinnamon and Szechuan pepper. It has an unmistakable flavour. Use it sparingly, as it is very pungent.

Aromatic lime leaves are used as a flavouring in this soup to add tartness.

Spicy Prawn Soup

SERVES 4

2 tbsp tamarind paste
4 fresh red chillies, chopped very finely
2 garlic cloves, crushed
2 tsp finely chopped fresh root ginger
4 tbsp fish sauce
2 tbsp palm sugar or caster sugar
1.25 litres/2 pints fish stock
8 lime leaves, torn roughly
100 g/3½ oz carrots, sliced thinly
350 g/12 oz sweet potato, diced
100 g/3½ oz baby corn cobs, halved
3 tbsp roughly chopped fresh coriander
100 g/3½ oz cherry tomatoes, halved
225 g/8 oz raw fan-tail prawns

1 Place the tamarind paste, red chillies, garlic, ginger, fish sauce, palm sugar and fish stock in a preheated wok or large, heavy-based saucepan. Add the lime leaves to the wok. Bring to the boil, stirring constantly, to blend the flavours.

2 Reduce the heat and add the carrot, sweet potato and baby corn cobs to the mixture in the wok.

3 Leave the soup to simmer, uncovered, for about 10 minutes, or until the vegetables are just tender.

4 Stir the coriander, cherry tomatoes and prawns into the soup and heat through for 5 minutes, until the prawns have changed colour

5 Transfer to a warm soup tureen or individual serving bowls and serve immediately.

NUTRITION

Calories 217; Sugars 16 g; Protein 16 g;
Carbohydrate 31 g; Fat 4 g; Saturates 1 g

⭐ very easy
◔ 10 mins
🕐 20 mins

🍳 COOK'S TIP

You could use Thai ginger or galangal, a member of the ginger family, instead of the root ginger in this recipe. It is yellow in colour with pink sprouts and a knobbly surface. The flavour is aromatic and less pungent than ginger.

Thai red curry paste is quite fiery, but adds a superb flavour to this dish. It is available in jars or packets from most supermarkets.

Coconut *and* Crab Soup

1 Heat the oil in a preheated wok or large, heavy-based saucepan.

2 Add the red curry paste and red pepper to the wok and stir-fry for 1 minute.

3 Add the coconut milk, fish stock and fish sauce and bring to the boil.

4 Add the crab meat, crab claws, coriander and spring onions to the wok.

5 Reduce the heat, stir the mixture well, and heat thoroughly for 2–3 minutes, or until everything has warmed through.

6 Transfer the soup to a warm soup tureen or individual serving bowls and serve immediately.

SERVES 4

1 tbsp groundnut oil
2 tbsp Thai red curry paste
1 red pepper, deseeded and sliced
600 ml/1 pint coconut milk
600 ml/1 pint fish stock
2 tbsp fish sauce
225 g/8 oz canned or fresh white crab meat
225 g/8 oz fresh or frozen crab claws
2 tbsp chopped fresh coriander
3 spring onions, trimmed and sliced

NUTRITION
Calories *122*; Sugar *9 g*; Protein *11 g*
Carbohydrates *11 g*; Fat *4 g*; Saturates *1 g*

 moderate

5 mins

10 mins

🍳 **COOK'S TIP**

Clean the wok by washing it with water, using a mild detergent, if necessary, and a soft cloth or brush. Do not scrub or use any abrasive cleaners as this will scratch the surface. Dry thoroughly, then wipe with a little oil.

Chinese mushrooms add an intense flavour to this soup. If you can't find them, use sliced, open-cap mushrooms instead.

Chilli Fish Soup

SERVES 4

15 g/½ oz Chinese dried mushrooms
2 tbsp sunflower oil
1 onion, sliced
100 g/3½ oz mangetout
100 g/3½ oz canned bamboo
　　shoots, drained
3 tbsp sweet chilli sauce
1.25 litres/2 pints fish or vegetable stock
3 tbsp light soy sauce
2 tbsp chopped fresh coriander, plus extra to
　　garnish (optional)
450 g/1 lb cod fillet, skinned and cubed

1　Place the mushrooms in a large bowl. Pour over enough boiling water to cover and leave to stand for 5 minutes. Drain the mushrooms thoroughly in a colander. Using a sharp knife, roughly chop the mushrooms.

2　Heat the sunflower oil in a preheated wok or large, heavy-based saucepan. Add the onion to the wok and stir-fry for 5 minutes, or until softened.

3　Add the mangetout, bamboo shoots, chilli sauce, stock and soy sauce to the wok and bring to the boil.

4　Reduce the heat, add the coriander and cod and simmer for 5 minutes, or until the fish is cooked through.

5　Transfer to a warm soup tureen or individual serving bowls, garnish with extra coriander, if using, and serve immediately.

NUTRITION
Calories *166*; Sugars *1 g*; Protein *23 g*;
Carbohydrate *4 g*; Fat *7 g*; Saturates *1 g*

very easy

15 mins

15 mins

🍳 COOK'S TIP

There are many different varieties of dried mushrooms, but shiitake are best in this dish. They are not cheap, but a small amount will go a long way.

This soup is an interesting mix of colours and textures. It is substantial enough to serve as a light meal in itself.

Prawn Soup

1 Heat the oil in a preheated wok or large, heavy-based saucepan until really hot. Add the spring onions and stir-fry for 1 minute, then add the carrot and mushrooms and continue to cook for about 2 minutes.

2 Add the stock and bring to the boil, then season to taste with salt and pepper, Chinese five-spice powder and soy sauce. Reduce the heat and simmer for 5 minutes.

3 If the prawns are really large, cut them in half (leaving 4 whole, to garnish) before adding to the wok. Simmer for 3–4 minutes, until they change colour.

4 Add the watercress to the wok and mix well, then slowly pour in the beaten egg in a circular movement so that it cooks in threads in the soup. Adjust the seasoning and serve each portion topped with a whole prawn.

SERVES 4

2 tbsp sunflower oil

2 spring onions, sliced thinly diagonally

1 carrot, grated roughly

125 g/4½ oz large closed-cup mushrooms, sliced thinly

1 litre/1¾ pints fish or vegetable stock

½ tsp Chinese five-spice powder

1 tbsp light soy sauce

125 g/4½ oz large raw, peeled prawns or tiger prawns, defrosted if frozen

½ bunch watercress, chopped roughly

1 egg, beaten well

salt and pepper

NUTRITION

Calories *123*; Sugars *0.2 g*; Protein *13 g*; Carbohydrate *1 g*; Fat *8 g*; Saturates *1 g*

⭐⭐   easy

🕐   5 mins

🕐   20 mins

👨‍🍳 **COOK'S TIP**

The egg may be made into a flat omelette and added as thin strips, if preferred.

Quick to make, this hot and spicy soup is hearty and warming. If you like your food really fiery, add a chopped dried or fresh chilli with its seeds.

Chicken Noodle Soup

SERVES 4

1 sheet dried egg noodles from a
   250 g/9 oz packet
1 tbsp sunflower oil
4 skinless, boneless chicken thighs, diced
1 bunch spring onions, sliced
2 garlic cloves, chopped
2 tsp finely chopped fresh root ginger
850 ml/1½ pints chicken stock
200 ml/7 fl oz coconut milk
3 tsp Thai red curry paste
3 tbsp peanut butter
2 tbsp light soy sauce
1 small red pepper, chopped
55 g/2 oz frozen peas
salt and pepper

1 Put the noodles in a shallow bowl and pour enough boiling water over to cover. Leave to stand as directed on the packet, then drain well.

2 Heat the oil in a preheated wok or large, heavy-based saucepan.

3 Add the chicken to the wok and stir-fry for 5 minutes, stirring constantly until lightly browned.

4 Add the white part of the spring onions, reserving the green parts, the garlic and ginger and stir-fry for a further 2 minutes.

5 Stir in the chicken stock, coconut milk, red curry paste, peanut butter and soy sauce, then bring to the boil.

6 Season with salt and pepper to taste. Reduce the heat, then simmer, for 8 minutes, stirring occasionally.

7 Add the red pepper, peas and green spring onion tops and simmer for a further 2 minutes.

8 Add the drained noodles and heat through. Spoon the soup into a warm soup tureen or individual serving bowls and serve with a spoon and fork.

NUTRITION

Calories 140; Sugars 3 g; Protein 3 g; Carbohydrate 20 g; Fat 17 g; Saturates 1 g

easy

15 mins

25 mins

🍳 COOK'S TIP

Thai green curry paste can be used instead of Thai red curry paste for a less fiery flavour.

Polenta (cornmeal) can be found in most supermarkets or health food shops. Yellow in colour, polenta acts as a binding agent in this spicy recipe.

Spicy Sweetcorn Fritters

1 Place the sweetcorn, chillies, garlic, lime leaves, coriander, egg and polenta in a large mixing bowl, and stir to combine.

2 Add the green beans to the ingredients in the bowl and mix well, using a wooden spoon.

3 Divide the mixture into small, evenly sized balls. Flatten the balls of mixture between the palms of your hands to form rounds.

4 Heat a little groundnut oil in a preheated wok or large, heavy-based frying pan until really hot. Cook the fritters, in batches, until brown and crispy on the outside, turning occasionally.

5 Leave the fritters to drain on absorbent kitchen paper, while frying the remaining fritters.

6 Transfer the drained fritters to warm serving plates and serve immediately.

SERVES 4

225 g/8 oz canned or frozen sweetcorn kernels
2 fresh red chillies, deseeded and chopped finely
2 garlic cloves, crushed
10 lime leaves, chopped finely
2 tbsp chopped fresh coriander
1 large egg
75 g/2¾ oz polenta
100 g/3½ oz fine green beans, sliced finely
groundnut oil, for frying

NUTRITION

Calories 213; Sugars 6 g; Protein 5 g; Carbohydrate 30 g; Fat 8 g; Saturates 1 g

⭐⭐ easy
◔ 5 mins
🕐 15 mins

👨‍🍳 **COOK'S TIP**

Kaffir lime leaves are dark green, glossy leaves that have a lemony-lime flavour. They can be bought, fresh or dried, from specialist Asian stores and some supermarkets. Fresh leaves impart the most delicious flavour.

This is a really simple dish, which is perfect served with a hot chilli dip.

Seven-spice Aubergines

SERVES 4

450 g/1 lb aubergines, sliced thinly
1 egg white
3½ tbsp cornflour
1 tsp salt
1 tbsp Chinese seven-spice powder
oil, for deep-frying

1 Place the aubergine in a colander, sprinkle with salt and leave to stand for 30 minutes. (This will remove all the bitter juices.)

2 Rinse the aubergine thoroughly and pat dry with absorbent kitchen paper.

3 Place the egg white in a small bowl and whip until light and foamy.

4 Using a spoon, mix together the cornflour, salt and Chinese seven-spice powder on a large plate.

5 Heat the oil for deep-frying in a preheated wok or large, heavy-based frying pan until very hot.

6 Dip the aubergine slices into the egg white, and then into the cornflour and seven-spice mixture to coat evenly.

7 Deep-fry the aubergine slices, in batches, for 5 minutes, or until pale golden and crispy.

8 Transfer the aubergines to kitchen paper and leave to drain. Arrange on serving plates and serve hot.

NUTRITION
Calories *169*; Sugars *2 g*; Protein *2 g*;
Carbohydrate *15 g*; Fat *12 g*; Saturates *1 g*

 very easy

35 mins

20 mins

COOK'S TIP

The best oil to use for deep-frying is groundnut oil which has a high smoking point and a mild flavour, so it will neither burn nor taint the food. About 600 ml/1 pint of oil is sufficient.

This is a very sociable dish if put in the centre of the table where people can help themselves, picking up and dipping pieces using cocktail sticks.

Fried Tofu *with* Peanut Sauce

1 Combine the rice wine vinegar, sugar and salt in a saucepan, then bring to the boil. Reduce the heat and simmer for 2 minutes.

2 Remove the sauce from the heat and add the peanut butter, chilli flakes and barbecue sauce, stirring well until thoroughly blended.

3 To make the batter, sift the plain flour into a bowl, make a well in the centre and add the eggs. Draw in the flour, adding the milk slowly. Stir in the baking powder and chilli powder.

4 Heat both the sunflower oil and sesame oil in a deep-fat fryer or large saucepan until a light haze appears on the top.

5 Dip the tofu triangles into the batter, then deep-fry until golden brown. You may need to do this in batches. Drain on kitchen paper.

6 Transfer the tofu triangles to a serving dish and serve immediately with the peanut sauce.

SERVES 4

2 tbsp rice wine vinegar
2 tbsp sugar
1 tsp salt
3 tbsp smooth peanut butter
½ tsp dried chilli flakes
3 tbsp barbecue sauce
1 litre/1¾ pints sunflower oil
2 tbsp sesame oil
500 g/1 lb 2 oz marinated or plain tofu, cut into 2.5-cm/1-inch triangles

batter
4 tbsp plain flour
2 eggs, beaten
4 tbsp milk
½ tsp baking powder
½ tsp chilli powder

NUTRITION
Calories *140*; Sugars *3 g*; Protein *3 g*;
Carbohydrate *20 g*; Fat *17 g*; Saturates *1 g*

⭐⭐⭐ moderate
🍳 15 mins
🕐 20 mins

👨‍🍳 **COOK'S TIP**

Tofu is made from processed soya beans. It is white, with a soft cheese-like texture, and is sold in blocks, either fresh or vacuum-packed. Although it has a bland flavour, it absorbs the flavours of spices and sauces.

Serve these bite-sized chicken balls warm as a snack with drinks, or cold for a picnic, party or lunchbox treat.

Chicken Balls *with* Sauce

SERVES 4

3 tbsp vegetable oil

2 large skinless, boneless chicken breasts, cut into 2-cm/ ³⁄₄-inch pieces

2 shallots, chopped finely

½ celery stick, chopped finely

1 garlic clove, crushed

2 tbsp light soy sauce

1 small egg

1 bunch spring onions, cut into 5-cm/ 2-inch lengths

salt and pepper

spring onion tassels, to garnish

dipping sauce

3 tbsp dark soy sauce

1 tbsp rice wine

1 tsp sesame seeds

1 Heat half of the oil in a preheated wok or large, heavy-based frying pan and stir-fry the chicken over a high heat for 2–3 minutes, until golden. Remove the chicken from the pan with a slotted spoon and set aside.

2 Add the shallots, celery and garlic to the pan and stir-fry for 1–2 minutes, until softened, but not browned.

3 Place the chicken, shallots, celery and garlic in a food processor and process until finely minced. Add 1 tablespoon of the light soy sauce, just enough egg to make a fairly firm mixture, and salt and pepper.

4 Make the dipping sauce by mixing together the dark soy sauce, rice wine and sesame seeds; set aside.

5 Shape the chicken mixture into 16–18 walnut-sized balls. Heat the remaining oil in the wok and stir-fry the balls in small batches for 4–5 minutes, until golden brown. As each batch is cooked drain on kitchen paper and keep hot.

6 Stir-fry the spring onions for 1–2 minutes, until they begin to soften, then stir in the remaining light soy sauce. Serve the chicken balls and a bowl of dipping sauce on a platter, garnished with the spring onion tassels.

NUTRITION

Calories 214; Sugars 29 g; Protein 20 g; Carbohydrate 5 g; Fat 13 g; Saturates 2 g

⭐⭐ easy

10 mins

25 mins

This tasty Chinese starter is not all that it seems – the 'seaweed' is in fact thinly sliced pak choi which is fried, salted and tossed with pine kernels.

Crispy Seaweed

1 Heat the groundnut oil in a preheated wok or large, heavy-based saucepan.

2 Carefully add the pak choi leaves to the wok and fry for about 30 seconds, or until they shrivel up and become crispy. (You will probably need to do this in several batches, depending on the size of your wok.)

3 Remove the crispy 'seaweed' from the wok with a slotted spoon and drain on kitchen paper.

4 Transfer the crispy 'seaweed' to a large bowl and toss with the salt, sugar and pine kernels. Serve immediately on warm serving plates.

SERVES 4

850 ml/1½ pints groundnut oil, for deep-frying
1 kg/2 lb 4 oz pak choi, leaves shredded thinly
1 tsp salt
1 tbsp caster sugar
2½ tbsp toasted pine kernels

COOK'S TIP

Use Savoy cabbage instead of the pak choi if it is unavailable, drying the leaves thoroughly before frying.

NUTRITION
Calories 214; Sugars 14 g; Protein 6 g; Carbohydrate 15 g; Fat 15 g; Saturates 2 g

⭐ very easy
🕐 10 mins
🕐 5 mins

This makes a substantial starter, light lunch or supper dish. Serve with a colourful, crisp salad.

Thai-stuffed Omelette

SERVES 4

2 garlic cloves, chopped
4 black peppercorns
4 sprigs fresh coriander
2 tbsp vegetable oil
200 g/7 oz minced pork
2 spring onions, chopped
1 large, firm tomato, chopped
6 large eggs
1 tbsp fish sauce
½ tsp ground turmeric
mixed salad leaves, to serve

1 Place the garlic, peppercorns and coriander in a pestle and mortar and crush to make a smooth paste.

2 Heat 1 tablespoon of the oil in a preheated wok or large, heavy-based frying pan over a medium heat. Add the paste and fry for 1–2 minutes, until it just changes colour.

3 Add the pork and stir-fry until it is lightly browned. Add the spring onions and tomato, and stir-fry for a further 1 minute, then remove from the heat.

4 Heat the remaining oil in a small, heavy-based frying pan. Beat the eggs with the fish sauce and turmeric, then pour a quarter of the egg mixture into the pan. As the mixture begins to set, stir lightly to ensure that all the liquid egg sets sufficiently.

5 Spoon a quarter of the pork mixture down the centre of the omelette, then fold the sides inwards towards the centre, enclosing the filling. Make 3 more omelettes with the remaining egg and fill with the pork mixture.

6 Slide the omelettes on to warm serving plates and serve with the mixed salad leaves.

NUTRITION
Calories 250; Sugars 1 g; Protein 21 g; Carbohydrate 2 g; Fat 18 g; Saturates 4 g

very easy

10 mins

25 mins

COOK'S TIP

If you prefer, spread half of the pork mixture evenly over 1 omelette, then place a second omelette on top, without folding. Cut into slim wedges to serve.

These small fish cakes are quick to make and are delicious served with a chilli dip.

Thai-style Fish Cakes

1 Place the cod pieces in a food processor with the fish sauce, chillies, garlic, lime leaves, coriander, egg and plain flour. Process until chopped finely and spoon into a large mixing bowl.

2 Add the green beans to the cod mixture and mix well.

3 Divide the mixture into small balls. Flatten the balls between the palms of your hands to form rounds.

4 Heat a little oil in a preheated wok or large, heavy-based frying pan. Fry the fish cakes on both sides until brown and crispy on the outside.

5 Transfer the fish cakes to serving plates and serve hot.

SERVES **4**

450 g/1 lb cod fillets, skinned and cut into bite-sized pieces
2 tbsp fish sauce
2 fresh red Thai chillies, deseeded and finely chopped
2 garlic cloves, crushed
10 lime leaves, chopped finely
2 tbsp chopped fresh coriander
1 large egg
25 g/1 oz plain flour
100 g/3½ oz fine green beans, sliced finely
groundnut oil, for frying

NUTRITION
Calories *214*; Sugars *14 g*; Protein *6 g*; Carbohydrate *15 g*; Fat *15 g*; Saturates *2 g*

⭐   very easy
🕐   10 mins
🕐   20 mins

👨‍🍳 **COOK'S TIP**

Fish sauce is a salty, brown liquid which is a must for an authentic Thai flavour. It is used to salt and flavour dishes and is available from Asian food stores or some large supermarkets.

These small prawn bites are packed with the flavours of lime and coriander, and make a quick and tasty starter.

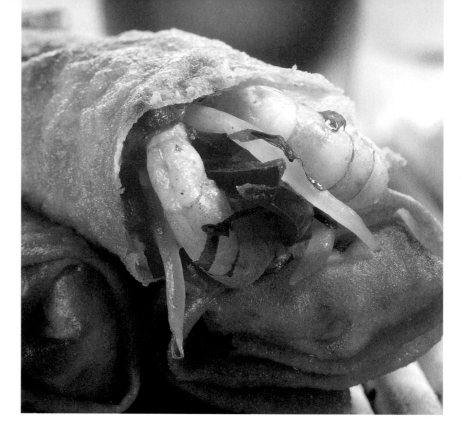

Prawn Parcels

SERVES 4

1 tbsp sunflower oil
1 red pepper, deseeded and sliced thinly
75 g/2¾ oz beansprouts
finely grated rind and juice of 1 lime
1 fresh red chilli, deseeded and
    chopped finely
1 tsp grated fresh root ginger
225 g/8 oz raw, peeled prawns
1 tbsp fish sauce
½ tsp arrowroot
2 tbsp chopped fresh coriander
8 sheets filo pastry
2 tbsp butter
2 tsp sesame oil
oil, for frying
chilli sauce, to serve

1 Heat the sunflower oil in a preheated wok or large, heavy-based frying pan. Add the red pepper and beansprouts and stir-fry for 2 minutes, or until the vegetables have softened.

2 Remove the wok from the heat and add the lime rind and juice, red chilli, ginger and prawns, stirring well.

3 Mix the fish sauce with the arrowroot and stir the mixture into the wok juices. Return the wok to the heat and cook, stirring, for 2 minutes, or until the juices thicken. Toss in the coriander and mix well.

4 Lay the sheets of filo pastry out on a board. Melt the butter and mix with the sesame oil and brush each pastry sheet with the mixture.

5 Spoon a little of the prawn filling on the bottom end of each sheet, fold over each side, and roll up to enclose the filling.

6 Heat the oil in a large wok. Cook the parcels, in batches, for 2–3 minutes, or until crisp and golden. Serve hot with a chilli dipping sauce.

NUTRITION
Calories *305*; Sugars *2 g*; Protein *15 g*;
Carbohydrate *14 g*; Fat *21 g*; Saturates *8 g*

⭐⭐⭐   moderate

🕐   15 mins

🕐   20 mins

🍳 **COOK'S TIP**

If using cooked rather than raw prawns, cook for just 1 minute, otherwise the prawns will become tough.

This is called *Fu Yong* in China and is a classic dish, which may be flavoured with any ingredients you have to hand.

Prawn Omelette

1 Heat the sunflower oil in a preheated wok or large, heavy-based frying pan. Add the leeks and stir-fry for 3 minutes.

2 Mix together the cornflour and salt in a large bowl.

3 Add the prawns to the cornflour and salt mixture and toss to coat all over.

4 Add the prawns to the wok or frying pan and stir-fry for 2 minutes, or until the prawns have changed colour and are almost cooked through.

5 Add the mushrooms and beansprouts to the wok and stir-fry for a further 2 minutes.

6 Beat the eggs with the water. Pour the egg mixture into the wok and cook until the egg sets, carefully turning the omelette over once. Turn the omelette out on to a clean board, divide into 4 and serve hot, garnished with deep-fried leeks, if using.

SERVES 4

3 tbsp sunflower oil
2 leeks, sliced
4 tbsp cornflour
1 tsp salt
350 g/12 oz raw, peeled tiger prawns
175 g/6 oz mushrooms, sliced
175 g/6 oz beansprouts
6 eggs
3 tbsp cold water
deep-fried leeks, to garnish (optional)

NUTRITION
Calories *320*; Sugars *1 g*; Protein *31 g*; Carbohydrate *8 g*; Fat *18 g*; Saturates *4 g*

 moderate

10 mins

10 mins

🧑‍🍳 **COOK'S TIP**

If liked, divide the mixture into 4 once the initial cooking has taken place in step 6, and make 4 individual omelettes.

These are one of the most recognised and popular starters in Chinese restaurants in the Western world. They are also quick and easy to make at home.

Sesame Prawn Toasts

SERVES 4

225 g/8 oz peeled, cooked prawns
1 tbsp soy sauce
2 garlic cloves, crushed
1 tbsp sesame oil
1 egg
4 slices medium-thick, sliced white bread, crusts removed (optional)
2 tbsp sesame seeds
oil, for deep-frying
sweet chilli sauce, to serve

1 Place the prawns, soy sauce, garlic, sesame oil and egg in a food processor and blend to make a smooth paste.

2 Spread the prawn paste evenly over the 4 slices of bread. Sprinkle the sesame seeds over the top of the prawn mixture and press the seeds into the paste with your hands so that they stick. Cut each slice into quarters to make 4 triangles.

3 Heat the oil in a preheated wok or large, heavy-based frying pan and deep-fry the toasts, sesame seed-side up, for 4–5 minutes, or until they are golden and crispy.

4 Remove the toasts with a slotted spoon, transfer to kitchen paper and leave to drain thoroughly.

5 Serve the toasts warm with sweet chilli sauce for dipping.

NUTRITION
Calories 237; Sugars 1 g; Protein 18 g;
Carbohydrate 15 g; Fat 12 g; Saturates 2 g

easy

5 mins

10 mins

🍲 **COOK'S TIP**

Add 2 chopped spring onions to the prawn mixture at the end of step 1 for more flavour.

Prawns are marinated in a soy sauce mixture, then coated in a light batter, fried and served with a delicious sweet-and-sour dip for a delicate starter.

Sweet *and* Sour Prawns

1 Using tweezers, de-vein the prawns, then flatten them with a large knife.

2 Place the prawns in a dish and add the ginger, garlic, spring onions, dry sherry, sesame oil and soy sauce. Cover with clingfilm and leave to marinate in the refrigerator for 30 minutes.

3 Make the batter by beating the egg whites until thick. Fold in the cornflour and plain flour to form a light batter.

4 Place the sauce ingredients in a saucepan and bring to the boil. Reduce the heat and simmer for 10 minutes.

5 Remove the prawns from the marinade and dip them into the batter to coat them evenly.

6 Heat the vegetable oil in a preheated wok or large, heavy-based frying pan until almost smoking. Reduce the heat and fry the prawns for 3–4 minutes, until crisp and golden brown.

7 Garnish the prawns with shredded spring onion and serve with the sauce.

SERVES 4

16 large peeled, raw prawns
1 tsp grated fresh root ginger
1 garlic clove, crushed
2 spring onions, sliced, plus extra to garnish
2 tbsp dry sherry
2 tsp sesame oil
1 tbsp light soy sauce
vegetable oil, for deep-frying

batter

4 egg whites
4 tbsp cornflour
2 tbsp plain flour

sauce

2 tbsp each tomato purée and lemon juice
3 tbsp white wine vinegar
4 tsp light soy sauce
3 tbsp light brown sugar
1 green pepper, deseeded and sliced thinly
½ tsp chilli sauce
300 ml/10 fl oz vegetable stock
2 tsp cornflour

NUTRITION
Calories *294*; Sugars *11 g*; Protein *14 g*; Fat *12 g*; Carbohydrate *34 g*; Saturates *2 g*

✪✪✪✪ challenging

40 mins

20 mins

Chicken wings make an ideal starter, since they are small and perfect for eating with the fingers.

Honeyed Chicken Wings

SERVES 4

450 g/1 lb chicken wings
2 tbsp peanut oil
2 tbsp light soy sauce
2 tbsp hoisin sauce
2 tbsp clear honey
2 garlic cloves, crushed
1 tsp sesame seeds

marinade
1 dried red chilli
½–1 tsp chilli powder
½–1 tsp ground ginger
finely grated rind of 1 lime

NUTRITION
Calories *131*; Sugars *4 g*; Protein *10 g*;
Carbohydrate *4 g*; Fat *8 g*; Saturates *2 g*

★★   easy
     2 hrs 5 mins
     40 mins

1 To make the marinade, crush the dried chilli in a pestle and mortar. Mix together the crushed dried chilli, chilli powder, ground ginger and lime rind in a small mixing bowl.

2 Thoroughly rub the spice mixture into the chicken wings with your fingertips. Leave the chicken wings to marinate in the refrigerator for at least 2 hours to allow the flavours to penetrate the meat.

3 Heat the peanut oil in a preheated wok or large, heavy-based frying pan.

4 Add the chicken wings and fry, turning frequently, for about 10–12 minutes, until golden and crisp. Drain off any excess oil.

5 Add the soy sauce, hoisin sauce, honey, garlic and sesame seeds to the wok, turning the chicken wings to coat.

6 Reduce the heat and cook for 20–25 minutes, turning the chicken wings frequently, until completely cooked through. Serve hot.

🍳 **COOK'S TIP**

Make the dish in advance and freeze the chicken wings. Defrost thoroughly, cover with foil and heat thoroughly in a moderate oven.

The dough used in this recipe may also be wrapped around chicken, pork, or prawns, or sweet fillings as an alternative.

Steamed Duck Buns

1 Place the duck breast in a large bowl. Mix together the light brown sugar, soy sauce, honey and hoisin sauce. Pour the mixture over the duck and marinate for 20 minutes.

2 Remove the duck from the marinade and cook on a rack set over a roasting tin in a preheated oven, 200°C/400°F/Gas Mark 6, for 35–40 minutes, or until cooked through. When cool, remove the meat from the bones and cut the meat into small cubes.

3 Heat the vegetable oil in a preheated wok or large, heavy-based frying pan. Add the leek, garlic and ginger and fry for 3 minutes. Mix with the duck.

4 Sift the plain flour into a large bowl. Mix the yeast, caster sugar and warm water in a separate bowl and leave in a warm place for 15 minutes.

5 Pour the yeast mixture into the flour, together with the warm milk, mixing to form a firm dough. Knead the dough on a floured surface for 5 minutes. Roll into a sausage shape, 2.5-cm/1-inch in diameter. Cut into 16 pieces, cover and leave to rest for 20–25 minutes.

6 Flatten the dough pieces into 10-cm/4-inch rounds. Place a spoonful of the duck mixture in the centre of each, draw up the sides to form a "moneybag" shape and twist to seal.

7 Place the dumplings on a clean, damp tea towel in the base of a steamer, cover and steam over a pan of gently simmering water for 20 minutes. Serve immediately.

SERVES 4

300 g/10½ oz duck breast
1 tbsp light brown sugar
1 tbsp light soy sauce
2 tbsp clear honey
1 tbsp hoisin sauce
1 tbsp vegetable oil
1 leek, chopped finely
1 garlic clove, crushed
1 tsp grated fresh root ginger

dough
300 g/10½ oz plain flour
15 g/½ oz dried yeast
1 tsp caster sugar
2 tbsp warm water
175 ml/6 fl oz warm milk

NUTRITION
Calories *307*; Sugars *11 g*; Protein *17 g*;
Carbohydrate *50 g*; Fat *6 g*; Saturates *1 g*

✪✪✪✪ challenging

1 hr 30 mins

1 hr

This classic Chinese dish is very popular in the West. Serve hot or chilled with a soy sauce or hoisin dip.

Spring Rolls

SERVES 4

175 g/6 oz cooked pork, chopped
75 g/2³/₄ oz cooked chicken, chopped
1 tsp each light soy sauce, light brown sugar, sesame oil and vegetable oil
225 g/8 oz beansprouts
25 g/1 oz canned bamboo shoots, chopped
1 green pepper, deseeded and chopped
2 spring onions, sliced
1 tsp cornflour
2 tsp water
vegetable oil, for deep-frying

skins

125 g/4¹/₂ oz plain flour
5 tbsp cornflour
450 ml/15 fl oz water
3 tbsp vegetable oil

NUTRITION

Calories *442*; Sugars *4 g*; Protein *23 g*;
Carbohydrate *42 g*; Fat *21 g*; Saturates *3 g*

⭐⭐⭐⭐ challenging
🕐 45 mins
🕐 30 mins

1 Mix together the pork, chicken, soy sauce, sugar and sesame oil in a bowl. Cover and marinate in the refrigerator for 30 minutes.

2 Heat the vegetable oil in a preheated wok or large, heavy-based frying pan. Add the beansprouts, bamboo shoots, green pepper and spring onions to the wok and stir-fry for 2–3 minutes. Add the meat and the marinade to the wok and stir-fry for 2–3 minutes.

3 Blend the cornflour with the water and stir the mixture into the wok. Set aside to cool completely.

4 To make the skins, combine the flour and cornflour and gradually stir in the water to make a smooth batter.

5 Heat a small, oiled frying pan. Swirl one-eighth of the batter over the base and cook for 2–3 minutes. Repeat with the remaining batter. Cover the skins with a damp tea towel while frying the remaining skins.

6 Spread out the skins and spoon one-eighth of the filling along the centre of each. Brush the edges with water and fold in the sides, then roll up.

7 Heat the oil for deep-frying in a wok to 180°C/350°F. Cook the spring rolls, in batches, for 2–3 minutes, or until golden and crisp. Remove from the oil with a slotted spoon, drain and serve immediately.

This classic dim sum dish is adaptable to almost any filling of your choice. Here, a traditional mixture of pork and pak choi is used.

Pancake Rolls

1 Heat the oil in a preheated wok or large, heavy-based frying pan. Add the garlic and stir-fry for 30 seconds. Add the pork and stir-fry for 2–3 minutes, until lightly coloured.

2 Add the pak choi, soy sauce and sesame oil to the wok and stir-fry for 2–3 minutes. Remove from the heat and set aside to cool.

3 Spread out the spring roll skins on a work surface and spoon 2 tablespoons of the pork mixture along one edge of each. Roll the skin over once and fold in the sides. Roll up completely to make a sausage shape, brushing the edges with a little water to seal. Set the pancake rolls aside for 10 minutes to seal firmly.

4 To make the chilli sauce, heat the sugar, vinegar and water in a small saucepan, stirring until the sugar dissolves. Bring the mixture to the boil and boil rapidly until a light syrup forms. Remove from the heat and stir in the red chillies. Leave the sauce to cool before serving.

5 Heat the oil for deep-frying in a wok until almost smoking. Reduce the heat slightly and fry the pancake rolls, in batches if necessary, for 3–4 minutes, until golden brown. Remove from the oil with a slotted spoon and drain on kitchen paper. Serve on warm serving plates with the chilli sauce.

SERVES 4

4 tsp vegetable oil
1–2 garlic cloves, crushed
225 g/8 oz minced pork
225 g/8 oz pak choi, shredded
4½ tsp light soy sauce
½ tsp sesame oil
8 spring roll skins, 25-cm/10-inches square, defrosted if frozen
oil, for deep-frying

chilli sauce
60 g/2 oz caster sugar
50 ml/2 fl oz rice wine vinegar
2 tbsp water
2 red chillies, chopped finely

NUTRITION
Calories *488*; Sugars *19 g*; Protein *16 g*; Carbohydrate *55 g*; Fat *24 g*; Saturates *4 g*

★★★★ challenging
 20 mins
20 mins

Poultry *and* Meat

Meat is expensive in Far Eastern countries and is eaten in smaller proportions than in the Western world. However, when meat is used, it is utilised to its full potential – it is marinated or spiced and combined with other delicious native flavourings to create a wide array of mouthwatering dishes. In Malaysia, a wide variety of spicy meats is offered, reflecting the many ethnic origins of the population. In China, poultry, lamb, beef or pork are stir-fried or steamed in the wok and combined with sauces and seasonings such as soy, black bean and oyster sauce. In Japan, meat is usually marinated and quickly stir-fried in a wok over a very high heat or simmered in miso stock. Thai dishes use meat that is leaner and more flavoursome due to its 'free-range' rearing.

The orange adds colour and piquancy to this refreshing dish, and is an ideal partner to chicken.

Stir-fried Ginger Chicken

SERVES 4

2 tbsp sunflower oil
1 onion, sliced
175 g/6 oz carrots, cut into matchsticks
1 garlic clove, crushed
350 g/12 oz skinless, boneless chicken breasts, cut into thin strips
2 tbsp grated fresh root ginger
1 tsp ground ginger
4 tbsp sweet sherry
1 tbsp tomato purée
1 tbsp demerara sugar
100 ml/3½ fl oz orange juice
1 tsp cornflour
1 orange, peeled and segmented
fresh snipped chives, to garnish

1 Heat the oil in a preheated wok or large, heavy-based frying pan. Add the onion, carrots and garlic and stir-fry over a high heat for 3 minutes, or until the vegetables begin to soften.

2 Add the chicken to the wok with the fresh and ground ginger. Stir-fry for a further 10 minutes, or until the chicken is well cooked through and golden in colour.

3 Mix together the sherry, tomato purée, sugar, orange juice and cornflour in a bowl. Stir the mixture into the wok and heat through until the mixture bubbles and the juices start to thicken.

4 Add the orange segments and carefully toss to mix.

5 Transfer the stir-fried chicken to warm serving bowls and garnish with fresh snipped chives. Serve immediately.

NUTRITION
Calories *289*; Sugars *15 g*; Protein *20 g*;
Carbohydrate *17 g*; Fat *9 g*; Saturates *2 g*

moderate

10 mins

20 mins

🍴 **COOK'S TIP**

Make sure that you do not continue cooking the dish once the orange segments have been added in step 4, otherwise they will break up.

Okra, or lady's fingers, are slightly bitter in flavour, although the pineapple and coconut in this recipe offset them in both colour and flavour.

Coconut Chicken Curry

1 Heat the oil in a preheated wok or large, heavy-based frying pan. Add the chicken to the wok and stir-fry until evenly browned.

2 Add the okra, onion and garlic to the wok and cook for for a further 2–3 minutes, stirring constantly.

3 Mix the curry paste with the chicken stock and lemon juice. Pour the mixture into the wok and bring to the boil. Reduce the heat, cover and simmer for 30 minutes.

4 Stir the grated coconut into the curry and cook for about 5 minutes.

5 Add the pineapple, yogurt and chopped coriander and cook for 2 minutes, stirring. serve with rice and garnish with sprigs of fresh coriander.

SERVES 4

2 tbsp sunflower oil

450 g/1 lb skinless, boneless chicken thighs or breasts, cut into bite-sized pieces

150 g/5½ oz okra, tops trimmed

1 large onion, sliced

2 garlic cloves, crushed

3 tbsp mild curry paste

300 ml/½ pint chicken stock

1 tbsp fresh lemon juice

100 g/3½ oz creamed coconut, grated roughly

175 g/6 oz fresh or canned pineapple, cubed

150 ml/5 fl oz thick, natural yogurt

2 tbsp chopped fresh coriander

freshly boiled rice, to serve

fresh coriander sprigs, to garnish

NUTRITION

Calories *456*; Sugars *21 g*; Protein *29 g*; Carbohydrate *22 g*; Fat *29 g*; Saturates *17 g*

★★★   moderate

🕐   5 mins

🕐   45 mins

 COOK'S TIP

Score around the top of the okra with a knife before cooking to release the sticky glue-like substance which is bitter in taste.

Yellow bean sauce is available from most large supermarkets. Try to buy a chunky sauce rather than a smooth one for added texture.

Cashew Chicken

SERVES 4

2 tbsp vegetable oil
450 g/1 lb skinless, boneless chicken breasts, cut into bite-sized pieces
1 red onion, sliced
175 g/6 oz flat mushrooms, sliced
100 g/3½ oz cashew nuts
75 g/2¾ oz jar yellow bean sauce
egg fried rice or plain boiled rice, to serve

1 Heat the vegetable oil in a preheated wok or large, heavy-based frying pan.

2 Add the chicken to the wok and stir-fry for 5 minutes.

3 Add the red onion and mushrooms to the wok and continue to stir-fry for a further 5 minutes.

4 Place the cashew nuts on a baking tray and toast under a preheated medium grill until just brown (toasting nuts brings out their flavour).

5 Toss the toasted cashew nuts into the wok together with the yellow bean sauce and heat through. Allow the sauce to bubble for 2–3 minutes.

6 Transfer the stir-fry to warm serving bowls and serve hot with egg-fried rice or plain boiled rice.

NUTRITION
Calories *398*; Sugars *2 g*; Protein *31 g*; Carbohydrate *8 g*; Fat *27 g*; Saturates *4 g*

easy

10 mins

15 mins

(🍳) **COOK'S TIP**

Chicken thighs could be used instead of the chicken breasts for a more economical dish.

This is on nearly everyone's list of favourite Chinese dishes, and it is so simple to make. Serve with stir-fried vegetables for a truly delicious meal.

Lemon Chicken

1 Heat the oil for deep-frying in a preheated wok or large saucepan to 180°C/350°F, or until a cube of bread browns in 30 seconds.

2 Reduce the heat and stir-fry the chicken strips for 3–4 minutes, until cooked.

3 Remove the chicken with a slotted spoon, set aside and keep warm. Drain the oil from the wok.

4 To make the sauce, mix the cornflour with 2 tablespoons of the water to form a paste.

5 Pour the lemon juice and remaining water into the wok.

6 Add the sweet sherry and caster sugar and bring to the boil, stirring until the sugar has completely dissolved.

7 Stir in the cornflour mixture and return to the boil. Reduce the heat and simmer, stirring constantly, for 2–3 minutes, until the sauce has thickened and cleared.

8 Transfer the chicken to a warm serving plate and pour the sauce over the top. Garnish with the lemon slices and shredded spring onion and serve.

COOK'S TIP

If you prefer to use chicken portions, rather than strips, cook them in the oil, covered, over a low heat for about 30 minutes, or until cooked through.

SERVES 4

vegetable oil, for deep-frying
650 g/1 lb 7 oz skinless, boneless chicken breasts, cut into strips

sauce

1 tbsp cornflour
6 tbsp cold water
3 tbsp fresh lemon juice
2 tbsp sweet sherry
½ tsp caster sugar

to garnish

lemon slices
shredded spring onion

NUTRITION

Calories 272; Sugars 1 g; Protein 36 g; Carbohydrate 5 g; Fat 11 g; Saturates 2 g

⭐⭐⭐ moderate

🕐 10 mins

🕐 15 mins

Chop suey is a well known and popular dish based on beansprouts and soy sauce with a meat or vegetable flavouring.

Chicken Chop Suey

SERVES 4

4 tbsp light soy sauce
2 tsp light brown sugar
500 g/1 lb 2 oz skinless, boneless, chicken
  breasts, cut into thin strips
3 tbsp vegetable oil
2 onions, quartered
2 garlic cloves, crushed
350 g/12 oz beansprouts
3 tsp sesame oil
1 tbsp cornflour
3 tbsp water
425 ml/15 fl oz chicken stock
shredded leek, to garnish

1 Mix the soy sauce and sugar together, stirring until the sugar has dissolved.

2 Place the chicken in a shallow dish and spoon the soy mixture over it, turning to coat. Marinate in the refrigerator for 20 minutes.

3 Heat the oil in a preheated wok or large, heavy-based frying pan. Add the chicken and stir-fry for 2–3 minutes, until golden brown. Add the onions and garlic and cook for a further 2 minutes. Add the beansprouts, stir-fry for 4–5 minutes, then add the sesame oil.

4 Mix the cornflour and water to form a smooth paste. Pour the stock into the wok, add the cornflour paste and bring to the boil, stirring until the sauce has thickened and cleared. Serve, garnished with the shredded leek.

NUTRITION

Calories *140*; Sugars *3 g*; Protein *3 g*;
Carbohydrate *20 g*; Fat *17 g*; Saturates *1 g*

⭐⭐⭐   moderate

🕐   25 mins

🕐   15 mins

👨‍🍳 COOK'S TIP

This recipe may be made with strips of lean steak, pork or mixed vegetables. Change the type of stock accordingly.

Chicken drumsticks are cooked in a delicious sauce and served with deep-fried basil for colour and flavour.

Chicken *with* Chilli *and* Basil

1 Remove the skin from the chicken drumsticks, if desired. Make 3 slashes in each drumstick. Brush the drumsticks with the soy sauce.

2 Heat the sunflower oil in a preheated wok or large, heavy-based frying pan and fry the drumsticks for 20 minutes, turning frequently, until they are cooked through.

3 Add the chilli, carrots and celery to the wok and cook for a further 5 minutes. Stir in the chilli sauce, cover and allow to bubble gently while preparing the basil leaves.

4 Heat a little oil in a heavy based frying pan. Carefully add the basil leaves – stand well away from the pan and protect your hand with a tea towel as they may spit a little. Cook the basil leaves for about 30 seconds, or until they begin to curl up, but not brown. Drain the leaves on kitchen paper.

5 Arrange the cooked chicken, vegetables and pan juices on to a warm serving plate, garnish with the crispy basil leaves and serve immediately.

SERVES 4

8 chicken drumsticks
2 tbsp soy sauce
1 tbsp sunflower oil
1 fresh red chilli, deseeded and chopped
100 g/3½ oz carrots, cut into matchsticks
6 celery sticks, cut into matchsticks
3 tbsp sweet chilli sauce
oil, for frying
about 50 fresh basil leaves

NUTRITION
Calories *196*; Sugars *2 g*; Protein *23 g*; Carbohydrate *3 g*; Fat *10 g*; Saturates *2 g*

moderate
10 mins
30 mins

🍳 **COOK'S TIP**

Basil has a very strong flavour, which is perfect with chicken and Chinese flavourings. You could use baby spinach instead of the basil, if you prefer.

In this recipe, the chicken is brushed with a glaze and deep-fried until golden. It is a little time-consuming, but well worth the effort.

Crispy Chicken

SERVES 4

1.5 kg/3 lb 5 oz oven-ready chicken
2 tbsp clear honey
2 tsp Chinese five-spice powder
2 tbsp rice wine vinegar
850 ml/1½ pints vegetable oil, for deep-frying
chilli sauce, to serve

NUTRITION

Calories 283; Sugars 8 g; Protein 29 g; Carbohydrate 8 g; Fat 15 g; Saturates 3 g

⭐⭐⭐⭐ challenging

🕐 15 hrs

🕐 35 mins

1 Rinse the chicken inside and out under cold running water and pat dry with kitchen paper.

2 Bring a large saucepan of water to the boil, then remove from the heat. Place the chicken in the water, cover and set aside for 20 minutes.

3 Remove the chicken from the boiled water and pat dry with kitchen paper. Leave to cool, then chill in the refrigerator overnight.

4 To make the glaze, mix together the honey, Chinese five-spice powder and rice wine vinegar in a small bowl.

5 Brush some of the glaze all over the chicken and return it to the refrigerator for 20 minutes.

6 Repeat this process of glazing and refrigerating the chicken until all of the glaze has been used up. Return the chicken to the refrigerator for at least 2 hours after the final coating.

7 Using a cleaver or heavy kitchen knife, open the chicken out by splitting it down the centre through the breast and then cut each half into 4 pieces.

8 Heat the oil for deep-frying in a preheated wok or large, heavy-based saucepan until almost smoking. Reduce the heat and fry each piece of chicken for 5–7 minutes, until golden and cooked through. Remove from the wok with a slotted spoon and drain on kitchen paper.

9 Transfer to a serving dish and serve hot with the chilli sauce.

This quick dish has many variations, but this version includes the classic combination of peanuts, chicken and chillies.

Spicy Peanut Chicken

1 Heat the peanut oil in a preheated wok or large, heavy-based frying pan.

2 Add the peanuts to the wok and stir-fry for 1 minute. Remove the peanuts with a slotted spoon and set aside.

3 Add the chicken to the wok and cook for 1–2 minutes.

4 Stir in the chilli and green pepper and cook for 1 minute. Remove the chicken, chilli and green pepper from the wok with a slotted spoon and set aside.

5 Put half of the peanuts in a food processor and process until almost smooth. If necessary, add a little stock to form a smoother paste. Alternatively, place them in a plastic bag and crush with a rolling pin.

6 To make the sauce, add the chicken stock, Chinese rice wine, light soy sauce, light brown sugar, garlic, ginger and rice wine vinegar to the wok.

7 Heat the sauce without boiling and stir in the peanut paste, the remaining peanuts, chicken, red chilli and green pepper. Mix well until all the ingredients are thoroughly combined.

8 Sprinkle the sesame oil into the wok, stir and cook for 1 minute. Transfer the chicken to a warm serving dish and serve immediately.

SERVES 4

2 tbsp peanut oil
125 g/4½ oz shelled peanuts
300 g/10½ oz skinless, boneless chicken breast, cut into 2.5-cm/1-inch cubes
1 fresh red chilli, sliced
1 green pepper, deseeded and cut into strips

sauce

150 ml/5 fl oz chicken stock
1 tbsp Chinese rice wine or dry sherry
1 tbsp light soy sauce
1½ tsp light brown sugar
2 garlic cloves, crushed
1 tsp grated fresh root ginger
1 tsp rice wine vinegar
1 tsp sesame oil

NUTRITION
Calories *342*; Sugars *3 g*; Protein *25 g*; Carbohydrate *6 g*; Fat *24 g*; Saturates *5 g*

★★★★ challenging
🕐 5 mins
🕐 10 mins

This is a refreshing dish suitable for a summer meal or light lunch.

Chinese Chicken Salad

SERVES 4

225 g/8 oz skinless, boneless chicken breasts
2 tsp light soy sauce
1 tsp sesame oil
1 tsp sesame seeds
2 tbsp vegetable oil
125 g/4½ oz beansprouts
1 red pepper, deseeded and thinly sliced
1 carrot, cut into matchsticks
3 baby corn cobs, sliced
2 tsp rice wine vinegar
1 tbsp light soy sauce
dash of chilli oil

to garnish
fresh chives
carrot matchsticks

1 Place the chicken breasts in a shallow glass dish.

2 Mix together the soy sauce and sesame oil and pour the mixture over the chicken. Sprinkle with the sesame seeds and leave to stand for 20 minutes, turning the chicken occasionally.

3 Remove the chicken from the marinade and cut the meat into thin slices.

4 Heat the vegetable oil in a preheated wok or large, heavy-based frying pan. Add the chicken and fry for 4–5 minutes, until cooked through and golden brown on both sides. Remove the chicken from the wok with a slotted spoon, set aside and leave to cool.

5 Add the beansprouts, red pepper, carrot and baby corn cobs to the wok and stir-fry for 2–3 minutes. Remove from the wok with a slotted spoon, set aside and leave to cool.

6 Mix together the rice wine vinegar, light soy sauce and chilli oil.

7 Arrange the chicken and vegetables together on a serving plate. Spoon the chilli oil mixture over the salad, garnish with chives and carrot and serve.

NUTRITION
Calories *162*; Sugars *3 g*; Protein *15 g*; Carbohydrate 5g; Fat *10 g*; Saturates *2 g*

⭐⭐ easy

🕐 25 mins

🕐 10 mins

Egg noodles are the ideal accompaniment to this quick dish, because they can be cooked quickly, while the stir-fry sizzles.

Speedy Peanut Pan-fry

1 Cook the noodles in a saucepan of lightly salted boiling water for 3–4 minutes, or following the packet directions. Drain the noodles well.

2 Meanwhile, heat the corn oil and sesame oil in a preheated wok or large, heavy-based frying pan. Add the chicken and stir-fry over a fairly high heat for 1 minute.

3 Add the courgettes, baby corn cobs and mushrooms and stir-fry for 5 minutes.

4 Add the beansprouts, peanut butter, soy sauce, lime juice and season with pepper to taste, then cook for a further 2 minutes.

5 Scatter the roasted peanuts over the noodles and serve with the courgette and mushroom mixture. Garnish with the sprigs of coriander and serve.

SERVES 4

250 g/9 oz dried thread egg noodles
2 tbsp corn oil
1 tbsp sesame oil
8 skinless, boneless chicken thighs or
    4 breasts, sliced thinly
300 g/10½ oz courgettes, sliced thinly
250 g/9 oz baby corn cobs, sliced thinly
300 g/10½ oz button mushrooms,
    sliced thinly
350 g/12 oz beansprouts
4 tbsp smooth peanut butter
2 tbsp soy sauce
2 tbsp lime or lemon juice
60 g/2 oz roasted peanuts
pepper
sprigs of fresh coriander, to garnish

NUTRITION
Calories 563; Sugars 7 g; Protein 45 g;
Carbohydrate 22 g; Fat 33 g; Saturates 7 g

★★ easy

🕐 5 mins

🕐 15 mins

 COOK'S TIP

Try serving this stir-fry with rice stick noodles as an alternative. These broad, pale, translucent ribbon noodles are made from ground rice.

This low-fat stir-fry features plenty of vegetables and healthy sunflower seeds, making it a quick, nutritious dish.

Chicken *and* Corn Sauté

SERVES 4

2 tbsp sunflower oil
4 skinless, boneless chicken breasts, sliced thinly
250 g/9 oz baby corn cobs, halved lengthways
250 g/9 oz mangetout
1 tbsp sherry vinegar
1 tbsp clear honey
1 tbsp light soy sauce
1 tbsp sunflower seeds
pepper
Chinese egg noodles or rice, to serve

1 Heat the sunflower oil in a preheated wok or large, heavy-based frying pan.

2 Add the chicken and stir-fry over a fairly high heat for 1 minute.

3 Add the baby corn cobs and mangetout and stir-fry over a moderate heat for 5–8 minutes, until the vegetables are still slightly crunchy and the chicken is cooked through.

4 Mix together the sherry vinegar, honey and soy sauce in a small bowl.

5 Stir the vinegar mixture into the pan with the sunflower seeds. Season well with pepper. Cook, stirring, for 1 minute.

6 Serve the dish hot with Chinese egg noodles or rice.

NUTRITION

Calories 280; Sugars 7 g; Protein 31 g; Carbohydrate 9 g; Fat 11 g; Saturates 2 g

easy

5 mins

10 mins

COOK'S TIP

Rice wine vinegar or balsamic vinegar may be used in place of sherry vinegar.

A colourful, exotic mix of flavours that works surprisingly well. This dish is easy and quick to cook – ideal for a mid-week family meal.

Chicken *and* Mango Stir-fry

1 Mix together the ginger, garlic and chilli in a shallow dish, then add the chicken and turn to coat evenly.

2 Heat the oil in a preheated wok or large, heavy-based frying pan over a high heat. Add the chicken and stir-fry for 4–5 minutes, until a light golden brown. Add the red pepper and stir-fry over a medium heat for 4–5 minutes, until softened.

3 Add the spring onions, mangetout and baby corn cobs and stir-fry for a further 1 minute.

4 Mix together the soy sauce, rice wine and sesame oil and pour the mixture into the wok. Add the mango and stir gently for 1 minute to heat thoroughly.

5 Season with salt and pepper to taste and serve immediately, garnished with fresh chives.

SERVES 4

2 tsp grated fresh root ginger
1 garlic clove, crushed
1 small fresh red chilli, deseeded
2 tbsp sunflower oil
6 skinless, boneless chicken thighs, cut into thin strips
1 large red pepper, deseeded and chopped
4 spring onions, sliced diagonally
200 g/7 oz mangetout, halved
100 g/3½ oz baby corn cobs, halved
1 tbsp light soy sauce
3 tbsp rice wine or sherry
1 tsp sesame oil
1 large mango, peeled and sliced thinly
salt and pepper
snipped fresh chives, to garnish

NUTRITION
Calories 200; Sugars 5 g; Protein 23 g;
Carbohydrate 7 g; Fat 6 g; Saturates 1 g

✪✪✪   moderate
🕐   10 mins
🕐   15 mins

Coconut adds a creamy texture and delicious flavour to this Thai-style stir-fry, which is spiked with green chilli.

Thai Stir-fried Chicken

SERVES 4

3 tbsp sesame oil
350 g/12 oz skinless, boneless chicken breasts, sliced thinly
8 shallots, sliced
2 garlic cloves, chopped finely
2 tsp grated fresh root ginger
1 fresh green chilli, chopped finely
1 each red and green pepper, sliced thinly
3 courgettes, sliced thinly
2 tbsp ground almonds
1 tsp ground cinnamon
1 tbsp oyster sauce
20 g/¾ oz creamed coconut, grated
salt and pepper

1 Heat the sesame oil in a preheated wok or large, heavy-based frying pan. Add the chicken, season with salt and pepper to taste, and stir-fry for about 4 minutes.

2 Add the shallots, garlic, ginger and chilli and stir-fry for 2 minutes.

3 Add the red and green peppers and courgettes and cook for about 1 minute.

4 Add the ground almonds, ground cinnamon, oyster sauce and creamed coconut and check the seasoning. Stir-fry for 1 minute and serve.

NUTRITION
Calories *184*; Sugars *6 g*; Protein *24 g*; Carbohydrate *8 g*; Fat *5 g*; Saturates *2 g*

 very easy

15 mins

10 mins

🍳 **COOK'S TIP**

Creamed coconut is sold in blocks by supermarkets and Oriental stores. It is a useful store-cupboard standby as it adds richness and depth of flavour.

This tasty chicken stir-fry is quick and easy to make and is full of fresh flavours and crunchy vegetables.

Chicken *with* Black Bean Sauce

1 Put the chicken in a bowl. Add the salt and cornflour and cover with water. Stir to combine and leave in the refrigerator for 30 minutes.

2 Heat 1 tablespoon of the oil in a preheated wok or large, heavy-based frying pan. Add the chicken and stir fry for 4 minutes.

3 Remove the chicken and transfer to a warm serving dish and clean the wok.

4 Add the remaining oil to the wok and add the garlic, black bean sauce, red and green peppers, chilli, mushrooms, onion and spring onions. Stir-fry for 2 minutes, then return the chicken to the wok.

5 Add the salt, sugar, chicken stock, dark soy sauce, beef stock and rice wine, then stir-fry for 3 minutes. Add the cornflour blend and cook until it has thickened and cleared. Serve with egg noodles.

SERVES 4

425 g/15 oz skinless, boneless chicken breasts, sliced thinly
pinch each of salt and cornflour
2 tbsp oil
1 garlic clove, crushed
1 tbsp black bean sauce
1 each small red and green pepper, deseeded and cut into strips
1 fresh red chilli, chopped finely
75 g/2¾ oz mushrooms, sliced
1 onion, chopped
6 spring onions, chopped
½ tsp each of salt and sugar
3 tbsp chicken stock
1 tbsp dark soy sauce
2 tbsp beef stock
2 tbsp Chinese rice wine
1 tsp cornflour, blended with a little Chinese rice wine
egg noodles, to serve

NUTRITION
Calories *184*; Sugars *6 g*; Protein *24 g*; Carbohydrate *8 g*; Fat *5 g*; Saturates *2 g*

✪✪✪   moderate

🕐   40 mins

🕐   10 mins

Traditional Christmas ingredients are given a Chinese twist in this stir-fry, which contains cranberries, ginger, chestnuts and soy sauce.

Turkey *with* Cranberry Glaze

SERVES 4

2 tbsp sunflower oil
1 skinless, boneless turkey breast, sliced thinly
15 g/½ oz stem ginger, chopped finely
50 g/1¾ oz fresh or frozen cranberries
100 g/3½ oz canned chestnuts
4 tbsp cranberry sauce
3 tbsp light soy sauce
salt and pepper

1 Heat the sunflower oil in a preheated wok or large, heavy-based frying pan.

2 Add the turkey to the wok and stir-fry for 5 minutes, or until cooked through.

3 Add the ginger and cranberries to the wok and stir-fry for 2–3 minutes, or until the cranberries have softened.

4 Add the chestnuts, cranberry sauce and soy sauce, season with salt and pepper to taste and allow to bubble for 2–3 minutes.

5 Transfer the turkey stir-fry to warm serving dishes and serve immediately.

NUTRITION
Calories *167*; Sugars *11 g*; Protein *8 g*;
Carbohydrate *20 g*; Fat *7 g*; Saturates *1 g*

easy
5 mins
15 mins

🍳 **COOK'S TIP**

It is very important that the wok is very hot before you begin to stir-fry. Test by holding your hand flat about 7.5 cm/3 inches above the base of the interior – you should be able to feel the heat radiating from it.

Chinese five-spice powder gives a lovely flavour to the duck, while the fresh chilli adds a slight kick.

Duck *in* Spicy Sauce

1 Heat the oil in a preheated wok or large, heavy-based frying pan. Reduce the heat slightly, add the ginger, garlic, chilli and duck and stir-fry for 2–3 minutes. Remove the duck from the wok and set aside.

2 Add the vegetables to the wok and stir-fry for 2–3 minutes. Pour off any excess oil from the wok and push the vegetables to one side.

3 Return the duck to the wok and pour in the stock. Sprinkle the Chinese five-spice powder over the top, stir in the rice wine and cook over a low heat for 15 minutes, or until the duck is tender.

4 Blend the cornflour with the water to form a paste and stir into the wok with the sesame oil. Bring to the boil, stirring until the sauce has thickened and cleared. Transfer the duck and spicy sauce to a warm serving dish and serve immediately.

SERVES 4

1 tbsp vegetable oil
1 tsp grated fresh root ginger
1 garlic clove, crushed
1 fresh red chilli, chopped
350 g/12 oz skinless, boneless duck meat, cut into strips
125 g/4½ oz cauliflower florets
55 g/2 oz mangetout
55 g/2 oz baby corn cobs, halved lengthways
300 ml/10 fl oz chicken stock
1 tsp Chinese five-spice powder
2 tsp Chinese rice wine or dry sherry
1 tsp cornflour
2 tsp water
1 tsp sesame oil

NUTRITION
Calories *162*; Sugars *2 g*; Protein *20 g*;
Carbohydrate *3 g*; Fat *7 g*; Saturates *2 g*

⭐⭐⭐   moderate

🕐   10 mins

🕐   25 mins

 COOK'S TIP

Omit the chilli for a milder dish, or deseed the chilli before adding it to the stir-fry to remove some of the heat.

Use fresh mangoes in this recipe for terrific flavour and colour. If they are unavailable, use canned mangoes and rinse them before using.

Duck *with* Mangoes

SERVES 4

2 ripe mangoes, peeled, stoned and cut into thin strips
300 ml/10 fl oz chicken stock
2 garlic cloves, crushed
1 tsp grated fresh root ginger
2 large skinless duck breasts, 225 g/8 oz each
3 tbsp vegetable oil
1 tsp rice wine vinegar
1 tsp light soy sauce
1 leek, cut into ribbons
chopped fresh parsley, to garnish

NUTRITION
Calories *235*; Sugars *6 g*; Protein *23 g*;
Carbohydrate *6 g*; Fat *14 g*; Saturates *2 g*

✪✪✪   moderate
🕐   10 mins
🕐   30 mins

1 Put half of the mango pieces and all of the chicken stock in a food processor and process until smooth. Alternatively, press half of the mangoes through a fine sieve and mix with the stock.

2 Rub the garlic and ginger over the duck. Heat the vegetable oil in a preheated wok or large, heavy-based fryng pan and cook the duck breasts, turning, until sealed. Reserve the oil in the wok and remove the duck.

3 Place the duck on a rack set over a roasting tin and cook in a preheated oven, 220°C/425°F/Gas Mark 7, for 20 minutes, until the duck is cooked through.

4 Meanwhile, place the mango and stock mixture in a saucepan and add the wine vinegar and light soy sauce.

5 Bring the mixture in the saucepan to the boil and cook over a high heat, stirring, until reduced by half.

6 Heat the oil reserved in the wok and stir-fry the leek and remaining mango for 1 minute. Remove from the wok, transfer to a serving dish and keep warm until needed.

7 Slice the cooked duck breasts and arrange on top of the leek and mango mixture. Pour the sauce over the duck, garnish with parsley and serve.

Duck is a strongly flavoured meat, which benefits from the addition of citrus peel to balance the richness.

Duck *with* Leek *and* Cabbage

1 Heat a wok or large, heavy-based frying pan and dry-fry the duck breasts, with the skin on, for about 5 minutes on each side (you may need to do this in 2 batches).

2 Remove the duck breasts from the wok and transfer to a clean board.

3 Using a sharp knife, cut the duck breasts into thin slices.

4 Remove all but 1 tablespoon of the fat from the duck left in the wok; discard the rest.

5 Add the green cabbage, leeks and orange rind to the wok and stir-fry for about 5 minutes, or until the vegetables have softened.

6 Return the duck to the wok and heat through for 2–3 minutes.

7 Drizzle the oyster sauce over the mixture in the wok, toss well to combine and heat through.

8 Transfer the stir-fry to warm serving dishes and serve sprinkled with toasted sesame seeds.

SERVES 4

4 duck breasts, 225 g/8 oz each
350 g/12 oz green cabbage, shredded thinly
225 g/8 oz leeks, sliced
finely grated rind of 1 orange
6 tbsp oyster sauce
1 tsp toasted sesame seeds, to serve

NUTRITION
Calories *140*; Sugars *3 g*; Protein *3 g*;
Carbohydrate *20 g*; Fat *17 g*; Saturates *1 g*

✪✪✪ moderate
🕐 15 mins
🕐 20–30 mins

🧑‍🍳 COOK'S TIP

Use thinly shredded Chinese leaves for a lighter, sweeter flavour instead of the green cabbage, if you prefer.

The pineapple and plum sauce add a sweetness and fruity flavour to this colourful recipe, which blends well with the duck.

Fruity Duck Stir-fry

SERVES 4

1 tsp Chinese five-spice powder
1 tbsp cornflour
1 tbsp chilli oil
4 duck breasts, sliced thinly
225 g/8 oz baby onions, peeled
2 garlic cloves, crushed
100 g/3½ oz baby corn cobs
175 g/6 oz canned pineapple chunks
6 spring onions, sliced
100 g/3½ oz beansprouts
2 tbsp plum sauce

1 Mix together the Chinese five-spice powder and the cornflour. Toss the duck in the mixture until well coated.

2 Heat the oil in a preheated wok or large, heavy-based frying pan. Stir-fry the duck for 10 minutes, or until crisp around the edges. Remove the duck from the wok and set aside.

3 Add the onions and garlic to the wok and stir-fry for 5 minutes, or until softened. Add the baby corn cobs and stir-fry for a further 5 minutes. Add the pineapple, spring onions and beansprouts and stir-fry for 3–4 minutes. Stir in the plum sauce.

4 Return the cooked duck to the wok and toss until well mixed. Transfer to warm serving dishes and serve hot.

NUTRITION
Calories 241; Sugars 7 g; Protein 26 g;
Carbohydrate 16 g; Fat 8 g; Saturates 2 g

★★   easy

        5 mins

        25 mins

  COOK'S TIP

Buy pineapple chunks in natural juice rather than syrup for a fresher flavour. If you can only obtain pineapple in syrup, rinse it in cold water and drain thoroughly before using.

Satay sauce is easy to make and is one of the best known and loved sauces in Oriental cooking. It is perfect with beef, chicken or pork.

Pork Satay Stir-fry

1 Heat the oil in a preheated wok or large, heavy-based frying pan. Add the pork, onion and garlic and stir-fry for 5 minutes, or until the pork is cooked through.

2 Add the carrots, yellow pepper, mangetout and asparagus to the wok and stir-fry for 5 minutes.

3 To make the satay sauce, place the peanut butter, coconut milk, chilli flakes, garlic and tomato purée in a small saucepan and heat gently, stirring, until well combined. (Be careful not to let the sauce stick to the bottom of the pan.)

4 Transfer the stir-fry to warm serving plates. Spoon the satay sauce over the stir-fry and scatter with chopped peanuts. Serve immediately.

SERVES 4

2 tbsp sunflower oil
350 g/12 oz pork neck fillet, sliced thinly
1 onion, sliced
2 garlic cloves, crushed
150 g/5½ oz carrots, cut into thin sticks
1 yellow pepper, deseeded and sliced
150 g/5½ oz mangetout
75 g/2¾ oz fine asparagus
chopped salted peanuts, to serve

satay sauce
6 tbsp crunchy peanut butter
6 tbsp coconut milk
1 tsp dried chilli flakes
1 garlic clove, crushed
1 tsp tomato purée

NUTRITION
Calories *506*; Sugars *11 g*; Protein *31 g*;
Carbohydrate *15 g*; Fat *36 g*; Saturates *8 g*

⭐⭐⭐   moderate

🕐   10 mins

🕐   15 mins

🍳 **COOK'S TIP**

Cook the sauce just before serving as it tends to thicken very quickly and will not be spoonable if you prepare it too far in advance.

Crisp, spicy pork is stirred into a delicious vegetable and egg rice for a very filling meal.

Spicy Pork *and* Rice

SERVES 4

275 g/9½ oz long-grain white rice
600 ml/1 pint cold water
2 tsp Chinese five-spice powder
4 tbsp cornflour
3 large eggs, beaten
25 g/1 oz demerara sugar
350 g/12 oz pork fillet, sliced thinly
2 tbsp sunflower oil
1 onion, diced
2 garlic cloves, crushed
100 g/3½ oz carrots, diced
1 red pepper, deseeded and diced
100 g/3½ oz frozen peas
2 tbsp butter
salt and pepper

NUTRITION
Calories *599*; Sugars *11 g*; Protein *30 g*;
Carbohydrate *76 g*; Fat *22 g*; Saturates *7 g*

✪✪✪✪ challenging

🕐 10 mins

🕐 35 mins

1 Rinse the rice under cold running water. Place the rice in a large saucepan, add the cold water and a pinch of salt, then bring to the boil. Reduce the heat, cover and simmer for about 9 minutes, or until all of the liquid has been absorbed and the rice is tender.

2 Whisk together the Chinese five-spice powder, cornflour, 1 egg and the demerara sugar. Toss the pork in the mixture until well coated.

3 Heat the sunflower oil in a preheated wok or large, heavy-based frying pan. Add the pork and stir-fry over a high heat until it is cooked through and crispy. Remove the pork from the wok with a slotted spoon and set aside until required.

4 Add the onion, garlic, carrots, pepper and peas to the wok and stir-fry for 5 minutes.

5 Return the pork to the wok, together with the cooked rice and stir-fry for 5 minutes.

6 Heat the butter in a frying pan. Add the remaining beaten eggs and swirl over the bottom of the pan to make an omelette. Cook until set, then turn out on to a clean board and thinly slice. Toss the strips of omelette into the rice mixture and serve immediately.

These small meatballs are packed with flavour and cooked in a tangy tomato sauce for a delicious meal.

Spicy Pork Balls

1 Place the minced pork in a large mixing bowl. Add the shallots, garlic, cumin seeds, chilli powder, breadcrumbs and beaten egg and mix together well.

2 Form the mixture into balls between the palms of your hands.

3 Heat the oil in a preheated wok or large, heavy-based frying pan. Add the pork balls and stir-fry, in batches, over a high heat for about 5 minutes, or until sealed on all sides. Remove from the wok and drain on kitchen paper.

4 Add the tomatoes, soy sauce and water chestnuts to the wok and bring to the boil. Return the pork balls to the wok, reduce the heat and simmer, stirring occasionally for 15 minutes.

5 Sprinkle with chopped fresh coriander and serve hot.

SERVES 4

450 g/1 lb minced pork
2 shallots, chopped finely
2 garlic cloves, crushed
1 tsp cumin seeds
½ tsp chilli powder
25 g/1 oz wholemeal breadcrumbs
1 egg, beaten
2 tbsp sunflower oil
400 g/14 oz canned chopped tomatoes, flavoured with chilli
2 tbsp soy sauce
200 g/7 oz canned water chestnuts, drained
3 tbsp chopped fresh coriander

NUTRITION
Calories 299; Sugars 3 g; Protein 28 g; Carbohydrate 14 g; Fat 15 g; Saturates 4 g

⭐⭐⭐⭐ challenging
🕐 10 mins
🕐 40 mins

COOK'S TIP

Add a few teaspoons of chilli sauce to a tin of chopped tomatoes, if you can't find the flavoured variety.

In this classic Chinese dish, tender pork pieces are fried and served in a crispy, fruity sauce. This dish is perfect with plain rice.

Sweet *and* Sour Pork

SERVES 4

2 tbsp sunflower oil
450 g/1 lb pork fillet, cut into bite-sized pieces
1 red onion, sliced thinly
2 garlic cloves, crushed
225 g/8 oz carrots, cut into thin sticks
225 g/8 oz courgettes, cut into thin sticks
1 red pepper, deseeded and sliced
100 g/3½ oz baby corn cobs
100 g/3½ oz button mushrooms, halved
175 g/6 oz fresh pineapple, cubed
100 g/3½ oz beansprouts
150 ml/5 fl oz pineapple juice
1 tbsp cornflour
2 tbsp soy sauce
3 tbsp tomato ketchup
1 tbsp white wine vinegar
1 tbsp clear honey

1 Heat the sunflower oil in a preheated wok or large, heavy-based frying pan. Add the pork to the wok and stir-fry for 10 minutes, or until the pork is completely cooked through and begins to crispen at the edges.

2 Add the onion, garlic, carrots, courgettes, red pepper, baby corn cobs and mushrooms to the wok and stir-fry for a further 5 minutes.

3 Add the pineapple and beansprouts to the wok and stir-fry for 2 minutes.

4 Mix together the pineapple juice, cornflour, soy sauce, tomato ketchup, white wine vinegar and honey.

5 Pour the sweet and sour mixture into the wok and cook over a high heat, tossing frequently, until the juices thicken. Transfer the pork to serving bowls and serve hot.

NUTRITION

Calories 357; Sugars 25 g; Protein 28 g; Carbohydrate 30 g; Fat 14 g; Saturates 4 g

★★★   moderate
     10 mins
     20 mins

COOK'S TIP

If you prefer a crisper coating, toss the pork in a mixture of cornflour and egg white and deep fry in the wok in step 2.

Mooli is a long, white root vegetable with a similar flavour to radish. It can be found in most large supermarkets.

Pork *with* Mooli

1 Heat 2 tablespoons of the vegetable oil in a preheated wok or large, heavy-based frying pan.

2 Add the pork to the wok and stir-fry for about 5 minutes.

3 Add the remaining vegetable oil to the wok. Add the aubergine to the wok together with the garlic and stir-fry for 5 minutes.

4 Add the mooli to the wok and stir-fry for about 2 minutes.

5 Stir the soy sauce and sweet chilli sauce into the mixture in the wok and cook until heated through.

6 Transfer the pork and mooli to warm serving bowls and serve immediately with boiled rice or noodles.

SERVES 4

4 tbsp vegetable oil

450 g/1 lb pork tenderloin, cut into bite-sized pieces

1 aubergine, diced

225 g/8 oz mooli, sliced

2 garlic cloves, crushed

3 tbsp soy sauce

2 tbsp sweet chilli sauce

boiled rice or noodles, to serve

NUTRITION

Calories *280*; Sugars *1 g*; Protein *25 g*; Carbohydrate *2 g*; Fat *19 g*; Saturates *4 g*

✪✪✪   moderate

     10 mins

     15 mins

This is a very simple dish, which lends itself to almost any combination of vegetables that you have to hand.

Pork *with* Vegetables

SERVES 4

2 tbsp vegetable oil
2 garlic cloves, crushed
1-cm/½-inch piece fresh root ginger, cut into slivers
350 g/12 oz lean pork fillet, sliced thinly
1 carrot, cut into thin strips
1 red pepper, deseeded and diced
1 fennel bulb, sliced
25 g/1 oz water chestnuts, halved
75 g/2¾ oz beansprouts
2 tbsp Chinese rice wine
300 ml/10 fl oz pork or chicken stock
pinch of dark brown sugar
1 tsp cornflour
2 tsp water

1 Heat the oil in a preheated wok or large, heavy-based frying pan. Add the garlic, ginger and pork and stir-fry for 1–2 minutes, until the meat is sealed.

2 Add the carrot, red pepper, fennel and water chestnuts to the wok and stir-fry for about 2–3 minutes.

3 Add the beansprouts and stir-fry for 1 minute. Remove the pork and vegetables from the wok with a slotted spoon and keep warm.

4 Add the Chinese rice wine or stock and sugar to the wok. Blend the cornflour to a smooth paste with the water and stir it into the sauce. Bring to the boil, stirring constantly until thickened and clear.

5 Return the meat and vegetables to the wok and cook for 1–2 minutes, until heated through and coated with the sauce. Serve immediately.

NUTRITION
Calories *216*; Sugars *3 g*; Protein *19 g*; Carbohydrate *5 g*; Fat *12 g*; Saturates *3 g*

moderate

5 mins

15 mins

COOK'S TIP

If you cannot find the Chinese rice wine use dry sherry instead.

Plum sauce is often used in Chinese cooking with duck or dark meat to balance the rich flavour of the meat.

Pork *with* Plums

1 Combine the cornflour, soy sauce, rice wine, light brown sugar and cinnamon in a small bowl.

2 Place the pork in a shallow dish and pour the cornflour mixture over it. Toss the meat in the marinade until it is completely coated. Cover and leave to marinate for at least 30 minutes.

3 Remove the pork from the dish, reserving the marinade.

4 Heat the oil in a preheated wok or large, heavy-based frying pan. Add the pork and stir-fry for 3–4 minutes, until a light golden colour.

5 Stir in the garlic, spring onions, plum sauce, hoisin sauce, water and chilli sauce. Bring the sauce to the boil. Reduce the heat, cover and simmer for 8–10 minutes, or until the pork is cooked through and tender.

6 Stir in the reserved marinade and cook, stirring, for about 5 minutes.

7 Transfer the pork stir-fry to a warm serving dish and garnish with fried plum quarters and spring onions. Serve immediately.

SERVES 4

1 tbsp cornflour
2 tbsp light soy sauce
2 tbsp Chinese rice wine
4 tsp light brown sugar
pinch of ground cinnamon
450 g/1 lb pork fillet, cut into thin slices
5 tsp vegetable oil
2 garlic cloves, crushed
2 spring onions, chopped
4 tbsp plum sauce
1 tbsp hoisin sauce
150 ml/5 fl oz water
dash of chilli sauce

to garnish
fried plum quarters
spring onion, sliced

NUTRITION
Calories *140*; Sugars *3 g*; Protein *3 g*;
Carbohydrate *20 g*; Fat *17 g*; Saturates *1 g*

✪✪✪   moderate
🕐   40 mins
🕐   20 mins

Small pieces of pork are coated in a light batter and deep-fried in this recipe – they are delicious dipped in a soy and honey sauce.

Deep-fried Pork Fritters

SERVES 4

2 tbsp peanut oil
450 g/1 lb pork fillet, cut into 2.5-cm/
    1-inch cubes
200 g/7 oz plain flour
2 tsp baking powder
1 egg, beaten
225 ml/8 fl oz milk
pinch of chilli powder
vegetable oil, for deep-frying
fresh chives, to garnish

sauce

2 tbsp dark soy sauce
3 tbsp clear honey
1 tbsp rice wine vinegar
1 tbsp chopped fresh chives
1 tbsp tomato purée

1 Heat the peanut oil in a preheated wok or large, heavy-based frying pan. Add the pork to the wok and stir-fry for 2–3 minutes, until sealed.

2 Remove the pork with a slotted spoon and set aside until required.

3 Sift the flour and baking powder into a mixing bowl and make a well in the centre. Gradually beat in the egg, milk and chilli powder to make a thick, smooth batter.

4 Heat the oil for deep-frying in a wok or large, heavy-based saucepan until almost smoking, then reduce the heat slightly.

5 Toss the pork pieces in the batter to coat thoroughly. Add the pork to the wok and deep-fry until golden brown and cooked through. Remove with a slotted spoon and drain well on kitchen paper.

6 Meanwhile make the sauce. Mix together all the ingredients and spoon into a small serving bowl.

7 Transfer the pork fritters to serving dishes, garnish with the chives and serve with the sauce.

NUTRITION

Calories 528; Sugars 12 g; Protein 32 g;
Carbohydrate 52 g; Fat 22 g; Saturates 6 g

✪✪✪   moderate

        15 mins

        20 mins

This classic dish features lamb marinated in chilli and coconut and threaded on to wooden skewers.

Lamb *with* Satay Sauce

1 Place the lamb in a large dish. Mix together the curry paste, coconut milk, garlic, chilli powder and cumin in a bowl. Pour the marinade over the lamb, toss well, cover and marinate in the refrigerator for 30 minutes.

2 To make the satay sauce. Heat the oil in a preheated wok or large, heavy-based frying pan and stir-fry the onion for 5 minutes, then reduce the heat and cook for 5 minutes.

3 Stir in the peanut butter, tomato purée, lime juice and water.

4 Thread the lamb on to wooden skewers, reserving the marinade.

5 Grill the lamb skewers under a hot grill for 6–8 minutes, turning once.

6 Add the reserved marinade to the sauce in the wok, bring to the boil and cook for 5 minutes. Serve the lamb skewers with the satay sauce.

SERVES 4

450 g/1 lb lamb loin fillet, sliced thinly
1 tbsp mild curry paste
150 ml/5 fl oz coconut milk
2 garlic cloves, crushed
½ tsp chilli powder
½ tsp ground cumin

satay sauce
1 tbsp corn oil
1 onion, diced
6 tbsp crunchy peanut butter
1 tsp tomato purée
1 tsp fresh lime juice
100 ml/3½ fl oz cold water

NUTRITION
Calories *501*; Sugars *6 g*; Protein *34 g*;
Carbohydrate *9 g*; Fat *37 g*; Saturates *10 g*

★★★   moderate
        35 mins
        25 mins

 COOK'S TIP

Soak the wooden skewers in cold water for 30 minutes before threading the lamb and grilling to prevent them from burning.

Red onions complement the colours of the sweet peppers in this dish – they taste good too.

Lamb *with* Black Bean Sauce

SERVES 4

1 egg white, beaten lightly

4 tbsp cornflour

1 tsp Chinese five-spice powder

450 g/1 lb lamb neck fillet or boneless leg of lamb, cut into thin strips

3 tbsp sunflower oil

1 red onion, sliced thinly

1 red pepper, deseeded and sliced

1 green pepper, deseeded and sliced

1 yellow or orange pepper, deseeded and sliced

5 tbsp black bean sauce

boiled rice or noodles, to serve

1 Mix together the egg white, cornflour and Chinese five-spice powder. Toss the lamb in the mixture until evenly coated.

2 Heat the oil in a preheated wok or large, heavy-based frying pan . Add the lamb and stir-fry over a high heat for 5 minutes, or until it becomes crisp around the edges.

3 Add the onion and red, green and yellow peppers to the wok and stir-fry for 5–6 minutes, or until the vegetables have softened.

4 Stir the black bean sauce into the mixture in the wok and heat through.

5 Transfer the lamb and sauce to warm serving plates and serve hot with boiled rice or noodles.

NUTRITION

Calories *328*; Sugars *5 g*; Protein *26 g*; Carbohydrate *12 g*; Fat *20 g*; Saturates *6 g*

   easy

10 mins

15 mins

🏵 COOK'S TIP

Take care when frying the lamb as the cornflour mixture may cause it to stick to the wok. Move the lamb around the wok constantly during stir-frying.

This really is a speedy dish, lamb leg steaks being perfect for the short cooking time.

Oyster Sauce Lamb

1 Sprinkle the ground Szechuan peppercorns over the lamb and toss together until well combined.

2 Heat the groundnut oil in a preheated wok or large, heavy-based frying pan.

3 Add the lamb to the wok and stir-fry for about 5 minutes.

4 Add the garlic and spring onions to the wok together with the dark soy sauce and stir-fry for 2 minutes.

5 Add the oyster sauce and Chinese leaves and stir-fry for a further 2 minutes, or until the leaves have wilted and the juices are bubbling.

6 Transfer the stir-fry to warm serving bowls and serve hot with prawn crackers, if liked.

SERVES 4

1 tsp ground Szechuan peppercorns
450 g/1 lb lamb leg steaks, sliced thinly
1 tbsp groundnut oil
2 garlic cloves, crushed
8 spring onions, sliced
2 tbsp dark soy sauce
6 tbsp oyster sauce
175 g/6 oz Chinese leaves, shredded
prawn crackers, to serve (optional)

NUTRITION
Calories 243; Sugars 0.4 g; Protein 26 g; Carbohydrate 3 g; Fat 14 g; Saturates 5 g

very easy

5 mins

10 mins

🍳 COOK'S TIP

Oyster sauce is made from oysters, which are cooked in brine and soy sauce. Sold in bottles, it will keep in the refrigerator for up to a month.

The long marinating time allows the garlic to penetrate the meat, creating a much more flavourful dish.

Garlic Lamb *with* Soy Sauce

SERVES 4

2 garlic cloves, sliced
450 g/1 lb lamb loin fillet, slashed
2 tbsp groundnut oil
3 tbsp dry sherry or Chinese rice wine
3 tbsp dark soy sauce
1 tsp cornflour
2 tbsp cold water
2 tbsp butter, cut into small pieces

1 Push the slices of garlic into the slits in the lamb. Place the garlic-infused lamb in a shallow dish.

2 In a small bowl, mix together 1 tablespoon each of the groundnut oil, dry sherry and dark soy sauce. Drizzle this mixture over the lamb, cover with clingfilm and leave to marinate in the refrigerator for at least 1 hour, preferably overnight.

3 Using a sharp knife or meat cleaver, thinly slice the marinated lamb.

4 Heat the remaining oil in a preheated wok or large, heavy-based frying pan. Add the marinated lamb and stir-fry for 5 minutes.

5 Add the marinade juices and the remaining sherry and soy sauce to the wok and allow the juices to bubble for 5 minutes.

6 Blend the cornflour to a smooth paste with the cold water. Add the cornflour mixture to the wok and cook, stirring occasionally, until the juices start to thicken and clear.

7 Add the butter to the wok or frying pan and stir until the butter melts. Transfer the lamb to serving dishes.

NUTRITION
Calories *309*; Sugars *0.2 g*; Protein *25 g*;
Carbohydrate *3 g*; Fat *21 g*; Saturates *9 g*

easy

1hr 15 mins

15 mins

Groundnut oil is used here for flavour; it is a popular oil for stir-frying because it has a high smoking point.

Lamb *with* Lime Leaves

1 Heat the oil in a preheated wok or large, heavy-based frying pan.

2 Add the garlic, shallots, lemon grass, lime leaves, tamarind paste, palm sugar and chillies to the wok and stir-fry for about 2 minutes.

3 Add the lamb and stir-fry for about 5 minutes, tossing well so that it is evenly coated in the spice mixture.

4 Stir the coconut milk into the wok and bring to the boil. Reduce the heat and simmer for 20 minutes.

5 Add the tomatoes and coriander to the wok and leave to simmer for 5 minutes. Transfer to serving plates and serve with fragrant rice.

SERVES 4

2 tbsp groundnut oil
2 garlic cloves, crushed
4 shallots, chopped
2 lemon grass stalks, sliced
6 lime leaves
1 tbsp tamarind paste
25 g/1 oz palm sugar
2 fresh red chillies, deseeded and
   chopped finely
450 g/1 lb lean leg of lamb or loin fillet,
   cut into bite-sized pieces
600 ml/1 pint coconut milk
175 g/6 oz cherry tomatoes, halved
1 tbsp chopped fresh coriander
cooked fragrant rice, to serve

NUTRITION
Calories *302*; Sugars *15 g*; Protein *24 g*;
Carbohydrate *17 g*; Fat *16 g*; Saturates *6 g*

★★★   moderate
       10 mins
       35 mins

🍳 **COOK'S TIP**

When buying fresh coriander, look for bright green, unwilted leaves. To store it, wash and dry the leaves, leaving them on the stem. Wrap the leaves in damp kitchen paper and keep them in a plastic bag in the refrigerator.

These small meatballs are made with minced lamb and flavoured with chilli, garlic, parsley and Chinese curry powder.

Lamb Meatballs

SERVES 4

450 g/1 lb minced lamb
3 garlic cloves, crushed
2 spring onions, chopped finely
½ tsp chilli powder
1 tsp Chinese curry powder
1 tbsp chopped fresh parsley
25 g/1 oz fresh white breadcrumbs
1 egg, beaten
3 tbsp vegetable oil
125 g/4½ oz Chinese leaves, shredded
1 leek, sliced
1 tbsp cornflour
2 tbsp water
300 ml/10 fl oz lamb stock
1 tbsp dark soy sauce
shredded leek, to garnish

1 Mix the lamb, garlic, spring onions, chilli powder, Chinese curry powder, parsley and breadcrumbs together in a bowl. Stir in the egg and combine to form a firm mixture. Using your hands roll into 16 small, even-sized balls.

2 Heat the oil in a preheated wok or large, heavy-based frying pan. Add the Chinese leaves and leek and stir-fry for 1 minute. Remove from the wok with a slotted spoon and set aside.

3 Add the meatballs to the wok and fry in batches, turning gently, for 3–4 minutes, or until golden brown all over.

4 Mix the cornflour and water together to form a smooth paste and set aside. Pour the lamb stock and soy sauce into the wok and cook for 2–3 minutes. Stir in the cornflour paste. Bring to the boil and cook, stirring constantly, until the sauce has thickened and cleared.

5 Return the Chinese leaves and leek to the wok and cook for 1 minute, until heated through. Arrange the Chinese leaves and leek on a warm serving dish, top with the meatballs and garnish with the shredded leek and serve.

NUTRITION
Calories 320; Sugars 1 g; Protein 28 g;
Carbohydrate 8 g; Fat 20 g; Saturates 6 g

✪✪✪ moderate
◔ 5 mins
◕ 20 mins

This curry uses the typically red-hot chilli flavour of Thai red curry paste, made with dried red chillies, which gives it a warm, russet-red colour.

Red Lamb Curry

1 Heat the oil in a preheated wok or large, heavy-based frying pan over a high heat and stir-fry the onion and garlic for 2–3 minutes, until softened. Add the lamb and fry the mixture quickly until lightly browned.

2 Stir in the curry paste and cook for a few seconds, then add the coconut milk and sugar and bring to the boil. Reduce the heat and simmer for 15 minutes, stirring occasionally.

3 Stir in the red pepper, stock, fish sauce and lime juice, cover and simmer for a further 15 minutes, or until the meat is tender.

4 Add the water chestnuts, coriander and basil, and season with salt and pepper to taste. Serve with jasmine rice, garnished with fresh basil leaves.

SERVES 4

2 tbsp vegetable oil
1 large onion, sliced
2 garlic cloves, crushed
500 g/1 lb 2 oz boneless lean leg of lamb, cut into 3-cm/1¼-inch cubes
2 tbsp Thai red curry paste
150 ml/5 fl oz coconut milk
1 tbsp soft light brown sugar
1 large red pepper, deseeded and thickly sliced
120 ml/4 fl oz lamb or beef stock
1 tbsp fish sauce
2 tbsp lime juice
225 g/8 oz canned water chestnuts, drained
2 tbsp chopped fresh coriander
2 tbsp chopped fresh basil
salt and pepper
boiled jasmine rice, to serve
fresh basil leaves, to garnish

NUTRITION
Calories *363*; Sugars *11 g*; Protein *29 g*; Carbohydrate *21 g*; Fat *19 g*; Saturates *6 g*

⭐⭐⭐   moderate
🕐   5 mins
🕐   40 mins

 COOK'S TIP

This curry can also be made with other lean red meats. Try replacing the lamb with trimmed duck breasts or pieces of lean braising beef.

This is a very simple, yet delicious dish, in which lean pieces of lamb are cooked in a sweet soy sauce and then sprinkled with sesame seeds.

Sesame Lamb Stir-fry

SERVES 4

2 tbsp peanut oil
450 g/1 lb boneless lean lamb, cut into thin strips
2 leeks, sliced
1 carrot, cut into matchsticks
2 garlic cloves, crushed
85 ml/3 fl oz lamb or vegetable stock
2 tsp light brown sugar
1 tbsp dark soy sauce
4½ tsp sesame seeds

1 Heat the peanut oil in a preheated wok or large, heavy-based frying pan until it is very hot.

2 Add the lamb and stir-fry for 2–3 minutes. Remove the lamb from the wok with a slotted spoon and set aside until required.

3 Add the leeks, carrot and garlic to the wok and stir-fry for 1–2 minutes.

4 Remove the vegetables from the wok with a slotted spoon and set aside.

5 Drain any remaining oil from the wok. Place the lamb stock, light brown sugar and dark soy sauce in the wok and add the lamb. Cook, stirring constantly for 2–3 minutes, until the lamb is coated in the mixture.

6 Sprinkle the sesame seeds over the top, turning the lamb to coat.

7 Spoon the leek, carrot and garlic mixture on to a warm serving dish and top with the lamb. Serve immediately.

NUTRITION
Calories 276; Sugars 4 g; Protein 25 g;
Carbohydrate 5 g; Fat 18 g; Saturates 6 g

easy

5 mins

10 mins

🍳 COOK'S TIP

Be careful not to burn the sugar in the wok when coating the meat, otherwise the flavour of the dish will be spoiled.

In this recipe, beef is marinated in a five-spice and garlic marinade for a rich, spicy flavour.

Spicy Beef

1 Mix together the garlic, star anise and dark soy sauce in a small bowl.

2 Pour the spice mixture over the steak, turning it to coat thoroughly. Cover and leave to marinate in the refrigerator for at least 1 hour.

3 To make the sauce, heat the oil in a preheated wok or large, heavy-based frying pan. Reduce the heat and stir-fry the spring onions for 1–2 minutes.

4 Remove the spring onions from the wok with a slotted spoon, drain on kitchen paper and set aside until required.

5 Add the beef to the wok with the marinade, and stir-fry for 3–4 minutes. Return the spring onions to the wok and add the soy sauce, sherry, chilli sauce and two thirds of the water.

6 Blend the cornflour with the remaining water and stir it into the wok. Bring to the boil, stirring, until the sauce has thickened and cleared.

7 Transfer to a warm serving dish and serve immediately.

SERVES 4

2 garlic cloves, crushed
1 tsp ground star anise
1 tbsp dark soy sauce
225 g/8 oz fillet steak, cut into thin strips

sauce
2 tbsp vegetable oil
1 bunch spring onions, halved lengthways
1 tbsp dark soy sauce
1 tbsp dry sherry
1/4 tsp chilli sauce
150 ml/5 fl oz water
2 tsp cornflour

NUTRITION
Calories *246*; Sugars *2 g*; Protein *21 g*;
Carbohydrate *10 g*; Fat *13 g*; Saturates *3 g*

★★   easy

           1 hr 15 mins

           20 mins

A fillet of beef is perfect for stir-fries as it is so tender and lends itself to quick cooking.

Stir-fried Beef *and* Vegetables

SERVES 4

2 tbsp sunflower oil
350 g/12 oz fillet of beef, sliced
1 red onion, sliced
175 g/6 oz carrots, sliced thinly
1 red pepper, deseeded and sliced
175 g/6 oz courgettes, sliced diagonally
1 small head Chinese leaves, shredded
150 g/5½ oz beansprouts
225 g/8 oz canned bamboo shoots, drained
150 g/5½ oz cashew nuts, toasted

sauce

3 tbsp medium sherry
3 tbsp light soy sauce
1 tsp ground ginger
1 garlic clove, crushed
1 tsp cornflour
1 tbsp tomato purée

1 Heat the sunflower oil in a preheated wok or large, heavy-based frying pan. Add the beef and red onion to the wok and stir-fry for about 4–5 minutes, or until the onion has softened and the meat begins to brown.

2 Add the carrots, red pepper, and courgettes to the wok and stir-fry for 5 minutes.

3 Toss in the Chinese leaves, beansprouts and bamboo shoots and heat through for 2–3 minutes, or until the leaves just begin to wilt.

4 Scatter the cashew nuts over the stir-fry and toss well to mix.

5 To make the sauce, mix together all the ingredients until well combined.

6 Pour the sauce over the stir-fry and toss to mix. Allow the sauce to bubble for 2–3 minutes, or until the juices thicken.

7 Transfer to warm serving bowls and serve at once.

NUTRITION
Calories 521; Sugars 7 g; Protein 31 g;
Carbohydrate 18 g; Fat 35 g; Saturates 8 g

moderate
10 mins
20 mins

Tender beef, marinated in a soy and tomato sauce, is stir-fried with crisp bamboo shoots and mangetout in this simple and tasty recipe.

Beef *with* Bamboo Shoots

1 Place the steak in a non-metallic dish with the dark soy sauce, tomato ketchup, garlic, lemon juice and ground coriander. Mix well to coat the meat in the marinade, cover and marinate in the refrigerator for at least 1 hour.

2 Heat the vegetable oil in a preheated wok or large, heavy-based frying pan. Add the meat to the wok and stir-fry for 2–4 minutes (depending on how well cooked you like your meat), or until cooked through.

3 Add the mangetout and bamboo shoots to the mixture in the wok and stir-fry over a high heat, tossing frequently, for a further 5 minutes.

4 Drizzle with the sesame oil and toss well to combine. Transfer to serving dishes and serve hot.

SERVES 4

350 g/12 oz rump steak, sliced thinly
3 tbsp dark soy sauce
1 tbsp tomato ketchup
2 garlic cloves, crushed
1 tbsp fresh lemon juice
1 tsp ground coriander
2 tbsp vegetable oil
175 g/6 oz mangetout
200 g/7 oz canned bamboo shoots
1 tsp sesame oil

COOK'S TIP

Leave the meat to marinate for at least 1 hour in order for the flavours to penetrate and increase the tenderness of the meat.

NUTRITION
Calories 275; Sugars 3 g; Protein 21 g; Carbohydrate 6 g; Fat 19 g; Saturates 6 g

easy

1 hr 15 mins

10 mins

It is unnecessary to use
expensive cuts of beef
steak for this recipe: the
meat will be tender, since
it is cut into small, thin
slices and marinated.

Beef *and* Black Bean Sauce

SERVES 4

250–300 g/9–10½ oz beef steak, such as
rump, cut into thin strips
about 300 ml/10 fl oz vegetable oil
1 spring onion, cut into short sections
a few small slices of fresh root ginger
1–2 small fresh green or red chillies,
deseeded and sliced
1 small onion, diced
1 small green pepper, deseeded and chopped
2 tbsp black bean sauce

marinade

½ tsp bicarbonate of soda or baking powder
½ tsp sugar
1 tbsp light soy sauce
2 tsp Chinese rice wine or dry sherry
2 tsp cornflour
2 tsp sesame oil

1 To make the marinade, mix together all the ingredients in a shallow dish. Add the beef, turn to coat and leave to marinate in the refrigerator for at least 2–3 hours.

2 Heat the vegetable oil in a preheated wok or large, heavy-based frying pan. Add the beef and stir-fry for about 1 minute, or until browned. Remove the beef with a slotted spoon and drain on kitchen paper. Keep warm and set aside until required.

3 Pour all but 1 tablespoon of the oil from the wok. Add the spring onion, ginger, chillies, onion and green pepper and stir-fry for about 1 minute.

4 Add the black bean sauce and stir until smooth. Return the beef to the wok, mix well and stir-fry for another minute. Transfer the stir-fry to a warm serving dish and serve hot.

NUTRITION

Calories *392*; Sugars *2 g*; Protein *13 g*;
Carbohydrate *3 g*; Fat *36 g*; Saturates *7 g*

easy

3hrs 15 mins

5 mins

COOK'S TIP

You could use chicken, turkey, lean pork, or even strips of venison instead of beef in this recipe.

Soy sauce and sesame seeds are classic ingredients in Chinese cooking. Use a dark soy sauce for a fuller flavour and richness.

Soy *and* Sesame Beef

1 Heat a wok or large, heavy-based frying pan until it is very hot.

2 Add the sesame seeds to the wok or frying pan and dry fry, stirring, for 1–2 minutes, or until they just begin to brown. Remove the sesame seeds from the wok and set aside until required.

3 Heat the vegetable oil in the wok. Add the beef and stir-fry for 2–3 minutes, or until sealed on all sides.

4 Add the green pepper and garlic to the wok and continue to stir-fry for 2 minutes.

5 Add the dry sherry and soy sauce to the wok with the spring onions. Allow the mixture to bubble, stirring occasionally, for about 1 minute, but do not let it burn.

6 Transfer the beef stir-fry to warm serving bowls and scatter with the dry-fried sesame seeds. Serve hot with egg noodles.

SERVES 4

2 tbsp sesame seeds
2 tbsp vegetable oil
450 g/1 lb beef fillet, sliced thinly
1 green pepper, deseeded and sliced thinly
4 garlic cloves, crushed
2 tbsp dry sherry
4 tbsp soy sauce
6 spring onions, sliced
boiled egg noodles, to serve

NUTRITION
Calories *324*; Sugars *2 g*; Protein *25 g*;
Carbohydrate *3 g*; Fat *22 g*; Saturates *6 g*

⭐⭐   easy
🕐   5 mins
🕐   10 mins

 COOK'S TIP

You can spread the sesame seeds out on a baking tray and toast them under a preheated grill until browned all over, if you prefer.

A delicately flavoured stir-fry infused with lemon grass and ginger. Colourful sweet peppers help to complete the dish.

Beef *with* Lemon Grass

SERVES 4

2 tbsp vegetable oil
1 garlic clove, chopped finely
500 g/1 lb 2 oz lean beef fillet, cut into long, thin strips across the grain
1 lemon grass stalk, shredded finely
2 tsp chopped finely fresh root ginger
1 red pepper, deseeded and thickly sliced
1 green pepper, deseeded and thickly sliced
1 onion, sliced thickly
2 tbsp lime juice
salt and pepper
boiled noodles or rice, to serve

1 Heat the oil in a preheated wok or large, heavy-based frying pan over a high heat. Add the garlic and stir-fry for 1 minute.

2 Add the beef and stir-fry for a further 2–3 minutes, until lightly coloured. Stir in the lemon grass and ginger and remove the wok from the heat.

3 Remove the beef from the wok with a slotted spoon and set aside. Add the red and green peppers and onion to the wok and stir-fry over a high heat for 2–3 minutes, until the onion is just turning golden brown and has slightly softened.

4 Return the beef to the pan, stir in the lime juice and season with salt and pepper to taste. Serve with noodles or rice.

NUTRITION

Calories 230; Sugars 4 g; Protein 26 g; Carbohydrate 6 g; Fat 12 g; Saturates 3 g

★★★ moderate
5 mins
10 mins

 COOK'S TIP

When preparing lemon grass, take care to remove the outer layers which can be tough. Use only the centre, tender part, which has the finest flavour.

The green of the beans complements the dark colour of the beef, which is served in a rich sauce.

Beef *and* Beans

1 Mix together the cornflour, soy sauce and peanut oil in a small bowl.

2 Place the steak in a shallow glass bowl. Pour the marinade over the steak, turn to coat thoroughly, cover and leave to marinate in the refrigerator for at least 30 minutes.

3 To make the sauce, heat the oil in a preheated wok or large, heavy-based frying pan. Add the garlic, onion, beans, cashew nuts and bamboo shoots and stir-fry for 2–3 minutes.

4 Remove the steak from the marinade, reserving the marinade and add the meat to the wok, then stir-fry for 3–4 minutes.

5 Mix together the soy sauce, Chinese rice wine and beef stock. Blend the cornflour with the water and add to the marinade, mixing well to combine.

6 Stir the mixture into the wok and bring the sauce to the boil, stirring until it has thickened and cleared. Reduce the heat and simmer for 2–3 minutes. Season with salt and pepper to taste and serve immediately.

SERVES 4

2 tsp cornflour
2 tbsp dark soy sauce
2 tsp peanut oil
450 g/1 lb rump or fillet steak, cut into 2.5-cm/1-inch pieces

sauce
2 tbsp vegetable oil
3 garlic cloves, crushed
1 small onion, cut into 8 pieces
225 g/8 oz green beans, halved
25 g/1 oz unsalted cashew nuts
25 g/1 oz canned bamboo shoots, drained and rinsed
2 tsp dark soy sauce
2 tsp Chinese rice wine or dry sherry
125 ml/4 fl oz beef stock
2 tsp cornflour
4 tsp water
salt and pepper

NUTRITION
Calories *381*; Sugars *3 g*; Protein *25 g*; Carbohydrate *10 g*; Fat *27 g*; Saturates *8 g*

easy
35 mins
15 mins

This recipe looks stunning if you arrange all the ingredients on a serving platter, rather than toss them together.

Beef *and* Peanut Salad

SERVES 4

½ head Chinese leaves, shredded
1 large carrot, cut into matchsticks
115 g/4 oz radishes, quartered
100 g/3½ oz baby corn cobs, halved lengthways
1 tbsp groundnut oil
1 fresh red chilli, deseeded and chopped
1 garlic clove, chopped finely
350 g/12 oz lean beef, such as fillet, sirloin or rump, shredded finely
1 tbsp dark soy sauce
25 g/1 oz fresh peanuts (optional)
fresh red chilli, sliced, to garnish

dressing

1 tbsp smooth peanut butter
1 tsp caster sugar
2 tbsp light soy sauce
1 tbsp sherry vinegar
salt and pepper

1 Arrange the Chinese leaves, carrot, radishes and baby corn corbs around the edge of a platter and set aside.

2 Heat the groundnut oil in a preheated wok or large, heavy-based frying pan until very hot.

3 Add the chilli, garlic and beef to the wok or frying pan and stir-fry for 5 minutes, until the meat has browned.

4 Add the dark soy sauce and stir-fry for a further 1–2 minutes, until the meat is tender and cooked through.

5 Meanwhile, make the dressing. Place all of the ingredients in a small bowl and blend them together until smooth.

6 Place the hot cooked beef in the centre of the salad ingredients. Spoon over the dressing and sprinkle with a few peanuts, if using. Garnish with slices of red chilli and serve immediately.

NUTRITION
Calories *194*; Sugars *3 g*; Protein *21 g*;
Carbohydrate *5 g*; Fat *10 g*; Saturates *3 g*

⭐⭐ easy
🕐 10 mins
🕐 10 mins

👨‍🍳 **COOK'S TIP**

You could use chicken, turkey, lean pork or even strips of venison instead of beef in this recipe.

A quick-and-easy stir-fry for any day of the week, this simple beef recipe is a good one-pan main dish.

Beef *with* Beansprouts

1 Heat the oil in a preheated wok or large, heavy-based frying pan over a high heat. Add the spring onions (reserving 2 spring onions, to garnish), the garlic and ginger and then stir-fry for 2–3 minutes, until softened. Add the beef and continue to stir-fry for 4–5 minutes, until browned evenly.

2 Add the red pepper and stir-fry for a further 3–4 minutes. Add the chilli and beansprouts and stir-fry for 2 minutes. Mix together the lemon grass, peanut butter, coconut milk, rice wine vinegar, soy sauce and sugar, then stir the mixture into the wok.

3 Meanwhile, cook the egg noodles in lightly salted boiling water for 4 minutes, or according to the packet directions. Drain the noodles and stir into the wok, tossing to mix evenly.

4 Season with salt and pepper to taste. Sprinkle with the reserved spring onions and serve hot.

SERVES 4

2 tbsp sunflower oil
1 bunch spring onions, sliced thinly
1 garlic clove, crushed
1 tsp chopped finely fresh root ginger
500 g/1 lb 2 oz tender beef, cut into thin strips
1 large red pepper, deseeded and sliced
1 small red chilli, deseeded and chopped
350 g/12 oz beansprouts
1 small lemon grass stalk, chopped finely
2 tbsp smooth peanut butter
4 tbsp coconut milk
1 tbsp rice wine vinegar
1 tbsp soy sauce
1 tsp soft light brown sugar
250 g/9 oz dried medium egg noodles
salt and pepper

NUTRITION
Calories *140*; Sugars *3 g*; Protein *3 g*; Fat *17 g*; Carbohydrate *20 g*; Saturates *1 g*

⭐⭐   easy
🕐   15 mins
🕐   20 mins

Fish *and* Seafood

Throughout the Far Eastern countries, fish and seafood play a major role in the diet of the native people; this is because these foods are both plentiful and very healthy. They are also very versatile: there are many different ways of cooking fish and seafood in a wok – they may be steamed, deep fried or stir-fried with a range of delicious spices and sauces.

Japan is famed for its sushimi, or raw fish, but this is just one of the wide range of fish dishes served. Fish and seafood are offered at every meal in Japan, many of them cooked in a wok.

When buying fish and seafood for the recipes in this chapter, freshness is imperative to flavour, so be sure to buy and use the fish that you have chosen as soon as possible, preferably on the same day as buying it.

Fish and fruit are a classic combination, and this dish is no exception with its tropical fruity flavour.

Stir-fried Cod *with* Mango

SERVES 4

2 tbsp vegetable oil
1 red onion, sliced
175 g/6 oz carrots, sliced thinly
1 red pepper, deseeded and sliced
1 green pepper, deseeded and sliced
450 g/1 lb skinless cod fillet, cubed
1 ripe mango, peeled, stoned and sliced
1 tsp cornflour
1 tbsp light soy sauce
100 ml/3½ fl oz tropical fruit juice
1 tbsp lime juice
1 tbsp chopped fresh coriander, to garnish

1 Heat the oil in a preheated wok or large, heavy-based frying pan. Add the onion, carrots and red and green peppers and stir-fry for 5 minutes.

2 Add the cod and mango to the wok and stir-fry for a further 4–5 minutes, or until the fish is cooked through. (Be careful not to break the fish up.)

3 Mix together the cornflour, soy sauce, fruit juice and lime juice. Pour the mixture into the wok and stir until the mixture bubbles and the juices thicken. Scatter with coriander and serve immediately.

NUTRITION

Calories *200*; Sugars *12 g*; Protein *21 g*;
Carbohydrate *14 g*; Fat *7 g*; Saturates *1 g*

★★   easy

🕐   10 mins

🕐   15 mins

🍳 COOK'S TIP

You can use paw-paw (papaya) as an alternative to the mango, if you prefer.

Szechuan pepper is quite hot and should be used sparingly to avoid making the dish too spicy.

Szechuan White Fish

1 Beat together the egg, flour, wine and 1 tablespoon of the soy sauce to make a batter. Dip the fish into the batter to coat well.

2 Heat the oil in a preheated wok or large, heavy-based frying pan. Reduce the heat slightly and cook the fish, in batches, for 2–3 minutes, until golden brown. Remove the fish with a slotted spoon, drain on kitchen paper, set aside and keep warm.

3 Pour all but 1 tablespoon of the oil from the wok and return it to the heat. Add the garlic, ginger, onion, celery, chilli and spring onions and stir-fry for 1–2 minutes. Stir in the remaining soy sauce and the rice wine vinegar.

4 Add the Szechuan pepper, fish stock and caster sugar to the wok. Mix the cornflour with the water to form a smooth paste and stir it into the stock. Bring to the boil and cook, stirring, for 1 minute, until the sauce thickens and clears.

5 Return the fish to the wok and cook for 1–2 minutes. Serve immediately.

SERVES 4

1 small egg, beaten
3 tbsp plain flour
4 tbsp dry white wine
3 tbsp light soy sauce
350 g/12 oz white fish fillets, cut into 4-cm/1½-inch cubes
vegetable oil, for frying
1 garlic clove, cut into slivers
1 tsp finely chopped fresh root ginger
1 onion, chopped finely
1 celery stick, chopped
1 fresh red chilli, chopped
3 spring onions, chopped
1 tsp rice wine vinegar
½ tsp ground Szechuan pepper
175 ml/6 fl oz fish stock
1 tsp caster sugar
1 tsp cornflour
2 tsp water

NUTRITION
Calories *140*; Sugars *3 g*; Protein *3 g*; Carbohydrate *20 g*; Fat *17 g*; Saturates *1 g*

★★   easy

    15 mins

    20 mins

This creamy fish curry is sensational with its Thai flavours of coconut, red curry paste and basil.

Fish *with* Coconut *and* Basil

SERVES 4

2 tbsp vegetable oil
25 g/1 oz seasoned flour
450 g/1 lb skinless cod fillet, cubed
1 garlic clove, crushed
2 tbsp Thai red curry paste
1 tbsp fish sauce
300 ml/10 fl oz coconut milk
175 g/6 oz cherry tomatoes, halved
20 fresh basil leaves, torn roughly
boiled fragrant rice, to serve

1 Heat the vegetable oil in a preheated wok or large, heavy-based frying pan.

2 Place the seasoned flour in a bowl. Add the cubes of fish and mix until well thoroughly coated.

3 Add the fish to the wok and stir-fry over a high heat for 3–4 minutes, or until the fish just begins to brown at the edges.

4 In a small bowl, mix together the garlic, curry paste, fish sauce and coconut milk. Pour the mixture over the fish and bring to the boil.

5 Reduce the heat, add the tomatoes to the mixture in the wok and simmer for 5 minutes.

6 Add the basil to the wok, stir carefully to combine, taking care not to break up the cubes of fish or tomatoes.

7 Transfer the curry to serving plates and serve hot with fragrant rice.

NUTRITION

Calories *209*; Sugars *10 g*; Protein *21 g*; Carbohydrate *15 g*; Fat *8 g*; Saturates *1 g*

moderate

5 mins

10 mins

🍲 COOK'S TIP

Take care not to overcook the dish once the tomatoes are added, otherwise they will break down and the skins will come away.

This is a very hot dish – not for the faint-hearted! It may also be made without the chilli, if preferred.

Crispy Fish

1 To make the batter, sift the plain flour into a mixing bowl and make a well in the centre. Add the egg yolk and peanut oil to the mixing bowl and gradually stir in the milk, incorporating the flour to form a smooth batter. Leave to stand for about 20 minutes.

2 Whisk the egg white until it forms soft peaks and fold it into the batter until thoroughly incorporated.

3 Heat the vegetable oil in a preheated wok or large, heavy-based frying pan. Dip the fish into the batter and fry, in batches, for 8–10 minutes, until cooked through. Remove the fish from the wok with a slotted spoon, drain on kitchen paper and keep warm until required.

4 Pour all but 1 tablespoon of the oil from the wok and return to the heat. Add the chilli, garlic, chilli powder, tomato purée, rice wine vinegar, soy sauce, Chinese rice wine, water and sugar and cook, stirring, for 3–4 minutes.

5 Return the fish to the wok and stir gently to coat it in the sauce. Cook for 2–3 minutes, until hot. Transfer to a serving dish and serve immediately.

SERVES 4

vegetable oil, for deep-frying
450 g/1 lb white fish fillets, cut into 2.5-cm/1-inch cubes

batter

55 g/2 oz plain flour
1 egg, separated
1 tbsp peanut oil
4 tbsp milk

sauce

1 fresh red chilli, chopped
2 garlic cloves, crushed
pinch of chilli powder
3 tbsp tomato purée
1 tbsp rice wine vinegar
2 tbsp dark soy sauce
2 tbsp Chinese rice wine
2 tbsp water
pinch of caster sugar

NUTRITION

Calories 281; Sugars 3 g; Protein 25 g; Carbohydrate 15 g; Fat 12 g; Saturates 2 g

moderate
30 mins
40 mins

This dish is a real treat and is perfect for special occasions. Monkfish has a tender flavour, which is ideal with asparagus, chilli and ginger.

Gingered Monkfish

SERVES 4

1 tbsp grated fresh root ginger
2 tbsp sweet chilli sauce
450 g/1 lb monkfish, cut into bite-sized pieces
1 tbsp corn oil
100 g/3½ oz fine asparagus
3 spring onions, sliced diagonally
1 tsp sesame oil

1 Mix together the ginger and sweet chilli sauce in a small bowl until thoroughly blended. Brush the ginger and chilli sauce mixture over the monkfish pieces, using a pastry brush.

2 Heat the corn oil in a large preheated wok or heavy-based frying pan.

3 Add the monkfish, asparagus and spring onions to the wok or frying pan and stir-fry for about 5 minutes, stirring gently so the fish pieces and asparagus do not break up.

4 Remove the wok or frying pan from the heat, drizzle the sesame oil over the stir-fry and toss well to combine.

5 Transfer the monkfish to warm serving plates and serve immediately.

NUTRITION
Calories 133; Sugars 0 g; Protein 21 g; Carbohydrate 1 g; Fat 5 g; Saturates 1 g

easy

5 mins

10 mins

COOK'S TIP

Monkfish is quite expensive, but it is well worth using as it has a wonderful flavour and texture. You could use cubes of chunky cod fillet instead.

Salmon is marinated in a deliciously rich, sweet sauce, stir-fried and served on a bed of crispy leeks.

Stir-fried Salmon *with* Leeks

1 Place the slices of salmon in a shallow non-metallic dish.

2 Mix together the soy sauce, tomato ketchup, rice wine vinegar, sugar and garlic in a small bowl.

3 Pour the soy sauce mixture over the salmon, toss well and leave to marinate in the refrigerator for about 30 minutes.

4 Meanwhile, heat 3 tablespoons of the corn oil in a preheated wok or large, heavy-based frying pan.

5 Add the leeks to the wok and stir-fry over a medium-high heat for about 10 minutes, or until the leeks become crispy and tender.

6 Using a slotted spoon, carefully remove the leeks from the wok and transfer to warmed serving plates.

7 Add the remaining oil to the wok. Add the salmon and the marinade to the wok and cook for 2 minutes.

8 Remove the salmon from the wok and arrange on top of the leeks, garnish with the red chillies and serve immediately.

SERVES 4

450 g/1 lb salmon fillet, skinned and sliced
2 tbsp sweet soy sauce
2 tbsp tomato ketchup
1 tsp rice wine vinegar
1 tbsp demerara sugar
1 garlic clove, crushed
4 tbsp corn oil
450 g/1 lb leeks, shredded thinly
finely chopped red chillies, to garnish

NUTRITION
Calories 360; Sugars 9 g; Protein 24 g; Carbohydrate 11 g; Fat 25 g; Saturates 4 g

⭐⭐ easy
40 mins
15 mins

Five-spice powder is a blend of star anise, fennel, cinnamon, cloves and Szechuan peppercorns. It is a popular addition to Chinese cooking.

Five-spice Salmon

SERVES 4

2 tsp Chinese five-spice powder
4 salmon fillets, 125 g/4½ oz each, skinned
1 large leek, shredded finely
1 large carrot, shredded finely
115 g/4 oz mangetout, shredded finely
2.5-cm/1-inch piece fresh root ginger, shredded finely
2 tbsp ginger wine
2 tbsp light soy sauce
1 tbsp vegetable oil
salt and pepper

to garnish
shredded leek
shredded fresh root ginger
shredded carrot

NUTRITION
Calories *267*; Sugars *3 g*; Protein *24 g*;
Carbohydrate *4 g*; Fat *17 g*; Saturates *3 g*

⭐⭐ easy

🕐 15 mins

🕐 6 mins

1 Rub the five-spice powder into both sides of the fish and season with salt and pepper. Set aside until required.

2 Place the vegetables in a large bowl and add the ginger, ginger wine and 1 tablespoon of the soy sauce.

3 Preheat the grill to medium. Place the salmon fillets on the grill rack and brush with the remaining soy sauce. Cook for 2–3 minutes on each side, until cooked through.

4 While the salmon is cooking, heat the oil in a preheated wok or large, heavy-based frying pan and stir-fry the vegetables for 5 minutes, until just tender. (Take care not to overcook the vegetables – they should still have bite.)

5 Transfer the vegetables to serving plates and place the salmon on top. Garnish with shredded leek, ginger and carrot and serve.

 COOK'S TIP

Chinese five-spice powder has a strong flavour and should be used sparingly.

The fish in this fragrant, curry-like stew can be varied according to taste or availability, but do stick to fish that stays firm when cooked.

Spicy Thai Seafood Stew

1 Heat the oil in a preheated wok or large, heavy-based frying pan and stir-fry the shallots, garlic and curry paste for 1–2 minutes. Add the lemon grass and shrimp paste, then stir in the coconut milk and bring to the boil.

2 Reduce the heat and add the white fish, squid and prawns to the wok and simmer for 2 minutes.

3 Add the clams and simmer for a further minute until the shells open. Discard any clams that do not open.

4 Scatter the shredded basil leaves over the stew, and serve immediately, garnished with whole basil leaves and fragrant rice.

SERVES 4

1 tbsp sunflower oil
4 shallots, chopped finely
2 garlic cloves, chopped finely
2 tbsp Thai green curry paste
2 small lemon grass stalks, chopped finely
1 tsp shrimp paste
500 ml/18 fl oz coconut milk
500 g/1 lb 2 oz firm white fish fillet, preferably monkfish or halibut, cut into bite-sized pieces
200 g/7 oz squid rings
200 g/7 oz raw, peeled tiger prawns
12 fresh clams in shells, cleaned
8 basil leaves, shredded finely
basil leaves, to garnish
boiled fragrant rice, to serve

NUTRITION
Calories 267; Sugars 7 g; Protein 42 g;
Carbohydrate 9 g; Fat 7 g; Saturates 1 g

 moderate

10 mins

10 mins

🧑‍🍳 COOK'S TIP

If you prefer, fresh mussels in shells can be used instead of clams – add them in Step 3 and follow the recipe as above.

Fresh tuna is a dark, meaty fish and is now widely available at fresh fish counters. It lends itself perfectly to the rich flavours in this recipe.

Tuna *and* Vegetable Stir-fry

SERVES 4

2 tbsp corn oil

1 onion, sliced thinly

225 g/8 oz carrots, shredded finely

175 g/6 oz mangetout

175 g/6 oz baby corn cobs, halved lengthways

450 g/1 lb fresh tuna, sliced thinly

2 tbsp fish sauce

1 tbsp palm sugar

finely grated rind and juice of 1 orange

2 tbsp sherry

1 tsp cornflour

boiled noodles or rice, to serve

1 Heat the corn oil in a preheated wok or large, heavy-based frying pan.

2 Add the onion, carrots, mangetout and baby corn cobs to the wok and stir-fry for 5 minutes.

3 Add the tuna to the wok and stir-fry for about 2–3 minutes, or until the tuna turns opaque.

4 Mix together the fish sauce, palm sugar, orange rind and juice, sherry and cornflour in a small bowl.

5 Pour the mixture over the tuna and vegetables and cook for 2 minutes, or until the juices thicken. Serve the stir-fry with noodles or rice.

NUTRITION

Calories *245*; Sugars *11 g*; Protein *30 g*; Carbohydrate *14 g*; Fat *7 g*; Saturates *1 g*

easy

10 mins

10 mins

🍳 COOK'S TIP

Try using swordfish steaks instead of the tuna. Swordfish steaks are now widely available and are similar in texture to tuna.

Fan-tail prawns give a special touch to a meal, especially when cooked in this delicious, crisp coconut coating.

Coconut Prawns

1 Mix together the desiccated coconut, white breadcrumbs, Chinese five-spice powder, salt and finely grated lime rind in a bowl.

2 Lightly whisk the egg white in a separate bowl.

3 Rinse the prawns under cold running water, and pat dry with kitchen paper.

4 Dip the prawns into the egg white then into the coconut and breadcrumb mixture, so that they are evenly coated.

5 Heat about 5-cm/2-inches of sunflower in a preheated wok or large, heavy-based frying pan.

6 Add the prawns to the wok and stir-fry for about 5 minutes, or until golden and crispy. Remove the prawns with a slotted spoon and leave to drain on kitchen paper.

7 Transfer the coconut prawns to warm serving dishes and garnish with lemon wedges. Serve immediately with soy or chilli sauce.

COOK'S TIP

Chinese five-spice powder will keep for a few months if stored in a cool, dark place in an airtight container.

SERVES 4

50 g/1¾ oz desiccated coconut
25 g/1 oz fresh white breadcrumbs
1 tsp Chinese five-spice powder
½ tsp salt
finely grated rind of 1 lime
1 egg white
450 g/1 lb raw fan-tail prawns
sunflower or corn oil, for frying
lemon wedges, to garnish
soy or chilli sauce, to serve

NUTRITION

Calories 236; Sugars 1 g; Protein 27 g; Carbohydrate 3 g; Fat 13 g; Saturates 7 g

easy

5 mins

10 mins

Hot and spicy, these prawns, coated in a crunchy batter, make a delicious starter or party food.

Szechuan Prawns

SERVES 4

pinch of salt
½ egg white, beaten lightly
1 tsp cornflour
250–300 g/9–10½ oz raw, peeled
   tiger prawns
600 ml/1 pint vegetable oil
fresh coriander leaves, to garnish

sauce

1 tsp chopped finely fresh root ginger
2 spring onions, chopped finely
1 garlic clove, chopped finely
3–4 small dried red chillies, deseeded
   and chopped
1 tbsp light soy sauce
1 tbsp tomato purée
1 tbsp oyster sauce
1 tsp Chinese rice wine or dry sherry
2–3 tbsp vegetable stock or water
few drops of sesame oil

NUTRITION
Calories *140*; Sugars *3 g*; Protein *3 g*;
Carbohydrate *20 g*; Fat *17 g*; Saturates *1 g*

easy

15 mins

15 mins

1 Mix together the salt, egg white and cornflour in a bowl. Dip the prawns in the mixture and turn until they are well coated.

2 Heat the oil in a preheated wok or large, heavy-based frying pan until it is smoking, then deep-fry the prawns for about 1 minute. Remove with a slotted spoon and drain on kitchen paper.

3 Pour off the oil, leaving about 1 tablespoon in the wok. Add all the ingredients for the sauce, in the order listed, bring to the boil and stir until smooth and well blended.

4 Reduce the heat, add the prawns to the sauce and stir until well blended.

5 Serve the prawns garnished with fresh coriander leaves.

COOK'S TIP

Raw prawns should be used if possible, but if unavailable use ready-cooked prawns and add at the beginning of step 3.

Basil and tomatoes are ideal partners for prawns, which, here, are also spiced with cumin seeds and garlic.

Prawns *with* Tomatoes

1 Heat the corn oil in a preheated wok or large, heavy-based frying pan.

2 Add the onion and garlic to the wok and stir-fry for 2–3 minutes, or until softened.

3 Stir in the cumin seeds and stir-fry for 1 minute.

4 Add the sugar, chopped tomatoes and sundried tomato purée to the wok. Bring the mixture to the boil, then reduce the heat and leave the sauce to simmer for 10 minutes.

5 Add the basil, prawns and salt and pepper to taste to the mixture in the wok. Increase the heat and cook for a further 2–3 minutes, or until the prawns are completely cooked through.

SERVES 4

2 tbsp corn oil
1 onion, chopped finely
2 garlic cloves, crushed
1 tsp cumin seeds
1 tbsp demerara sugar
400 g/14 oz canned chopped tomatoes
1 tbsp sundried tomato purée
1 tbsp chopped fresh basil
450 g/1 lb cooked, peeled king prawns
salt and pepper

NUTRITION
Calories *237*; Sugar *9 g*; Protein *27 g*; Carbohydrate *11 g*; Fat *10 g*; Saturates *1 g*

 ✪✪   easy

🕑   2 mins

🕐   20 mins

🍽 **COOK'S TIP**

Always heat your wok before you add oil or any other ingredients. This will prevent anything from sticking to it.

Crispy ginger is a wonderful garnish, which offsets the spicy prawns both visually and in flavour.

Prawns *with* Ginger

SERVES 4

oil, for frying
5-cm/2-inch piece fresh root ginger, cut into thin strips
1 onion, diced
225 g/8 oz carrots, diced
100 g/3½ oz frozen peas
100 g/3½ oz beansprouts
1 tsp Chinese five-spice powder
1 tbsp tomato purée
1 tbsp soy sauce
450 g/1 lb raw, peeled king prawns

1 Heat about 2.5-cm/1-inch of oil in a preheated wok or large, heavy-based frying pan. Add the ginger and stir-fry for 1 minute, or until crispy. Remove the ginger with a slotted spoon and leave to drain on kitchen paper.

2 Pour all but 2 tablespoons of the oil from the wok. Add the onion and carrots to the wok and stir-fry for 5 minutes. Add the peas and beansprouts and stir-fry for another 2 minutes.

3 Combine the Chinese five-spice powder, tomato purée and soy sauce. Brush the mixture over the prawns.

4 Add the prawns to the wok and stir-fry for a further 2 minutes, or until the prawns are completely cooked through. Transfer the prawn mixture to a warm serving bowl and top with the crispy ginger. Serve immediately.

NUTRITION
Calories *140*; Sugars *3 g*; Protein *3 g*;
Carbohydrate *20 g*; Fat *17 g*; Saturates *1 g*

easy

15 mins

15 mins

🍲 **COOK'S TIP**

Use slices of white fish instead of the king prawns, if you wish.

The classic ingredients of this popular dish are eggs, carrots and prawns. Add extra ingredients, such as peas or crab meat, if desired.

Prawn Fu Yong

1 Heat the vegetable oil in a preheated wok or large, heavy-based frying pan, swirling it around until it is very hot.

2 Add the carrot and stir-fry for 1–2 minutes, until just tender.

3 Push the carrot to one side of the wok and add the beaten eggs. Cook, stirring gently, for 1–2 minutes.

4 Stir the prawns, light soy sauce and Chinese five-spice powder into the mixture in the wok. Stir-fry for 2–3 minutes, or until the prawns change colour and the mixture is almost dry.

5 Spoon the prawn stir-fry on to warm plates and sprinkle the spring onions, sesame seeds and sesame oil on top. Serve immediately.

SERVES 4

2 tbsp vegetable oil
1 carrot, grated
5 eggs, beaten
225 g/8 oz raw, peeled prawns
1 tbsp light soy sauce
pinch of Chinese five-spice powder
2 spring onions, chopped
2 tsp sesame seeds
1 tsp sesame oil

NUTRITION
Calories 240; Sugars 1 g; Protein 22 g;
Carbohydrate 1 g; Fat 16 g; Saturates 3 g

easy
5 mins
10 mins

 COOK'S TIP

If only cooked prawns are available, add them just before the end of cooking, but make sure they are fully incorporated into the fu yong. They require only heating through, as overcooking will make them chewy and tasteless.

This prawn dish is very simple, and is ideal for supper or lunch when time is short.

Cantonese Prawns

SERVES 4

5 tbsp vegetable oil
4 garlic cloves, crushed
675 g/1½ lb raw, peeled prawns
4 tsp chopped fresh root ginger
175 g/6 oz lean pork, diced
1 leek, sliced
2 tbsp Chinese rice wine or dry sherry
2 tbsp light soy sauce
2 tsp caster sugar
150 ml/5 fl oz fish stock
4½ tsp cornflour
3 tbsp water
3 eggs, beaten

to garnish
shredded leek
red pepper matchsticks

NUTRITION
Calories *460*; Sugar *3 g*; Protein *53 g*;
Carbohydrate *6 g*; Fat *24 g*; Saturates *5 g*

★★★   moderate

◔   10 mins

🕐   20 mins

1 Heat 2 tablespoons of the vegetable oil in a preheated wok or large, heavy-based frying pan.

2 Add the garlic to the wok and stir-fry for 30 seconds.

3 Add the prawns to the wok and stir-fry for 5 minutes, or until they change colour. Remove the prawns from the wok with a slotted spoon, set aside and keep warm.

4 Add the remaining oil to the wok and heat, carefully swirling the oil around the base of the wok until it is really hot.

5 Add the ginger, pork and leek to the wok and stir-fry over a medium heat for 4–5 minutes, or until the pork is lightly coloured and sealed.

6 Add the rice wine, soy sauce, caster sugar and fish stock to the wok and stir to blend.

7 In a small bowl, blend the cornflour with the water to form a smooth paste and stir it into the wok. Cook, stirring, until the sauce thickens and clears.

8 Return the prawns to the wok and add the eggs. Cook for 5–6 minutes, gently stirring occasionally, until the eggs have set.

9 Transfer to a warm serving dish, garnish with shredded leek and pepper matchsticks and serve immediately with rice.

Scallops have a terrific, subtle flavour, which is complemented in this dish by the buttery sauce.

Seared Scallops

1 Heat the vegetable oil in a preheated wok or large, heavy-based frying pan, swirling the oil around the base of the wok until it is very hot.

2 Add the green chilli, spring onions and scallops to the wok and stir-fry over a high heat for 4–5 minutes, or until the scallops are just cooked through. If using frozen scallops, be sure not to overcook them, as they will begin to disintegrate.

3 Add the soy sauce and butter to the scallop stir-fry and heat through until the butter melts.

4 Transfer to warm serving bowls and serve hot.

SERVES 4

2 tbsp vegetable oil
1 fresh green chilli, deseeded and sliced
6 spring onions, sliced thinly
450 g/1 lb fresh scallops, without roe, or the same amount of frozen scallops, defrosted thoroughly and halved horizontally
3 tbsp sweet soy sauce
2 tbsp butter, cubed

NUTRITION
Calories 272; Sugars 0 g; Protein 28 g; Carbohydrate 2 g; Fat 17 g; Saturates 8 g

⭐ very easy
🕐 10 mins
🕐 10 mins

🧑‍🍳 **COOK'S TIP**

If you buy scallops on the shell, slide a knife underneath the membrane to loosen it and cut off the tough muscle that holds the scallop to the shell. Discard the black stomach sac and intestinal vein.

Scallops are both attractive and delicious. Cooked with ginger and orange, this dish is perfect served with plain rice.

Scallops *in* Ginger Sauce

SERVES 4

2 tbsp vegetable oil

450 g/1 lb fresh scallops, defrosted thoroughly, if frozen, cleaned and halved,

2 tsp chopped finely fresh root ginger

3 garlic cloves, crushed

2 leeks, shredded

75 g/2¾ oz frozen peas

125 g/4½ oz canned bamboo shoots, drained and rinsed

2 tbsp light soy sauce

2 tbsp unsweetened orange juice

1 tsp caster sugar

orange rind, to garnish

1 Heat the vegetable oil in a preheated wok or large, heavy-based frying pan. Add the scallops and stir-fry for 1–2 minutes. Remove the scallops from the wok with a slotted spoon, keep warm and set aside until required.

2 Add the ginger and garlic to the wok and stir-fry for 30 seconds. Stir in the leeks and peas and cook, stirring, for a further 2 minutes.

3 Add the bamboo shoots and return the scallops to the wok. Stir gently to mix without breaking up the scallops.

4 Stir in the soy sauce, orange juice and caster sugar and cook for 1–2 minutes.

5 Transfer the stir-fry to a serving dish, garnish with the orange rind and serve.

NUTRITION

Calories *216*; Sugars *4 g*; Protein *30 g*; Carbohydrate *8 g*; Fat *8 g*; Saturates *1 g*

⭐⭐ easy

🕐 5 mins

🕐 10 mins

 COOK'S TIP

The edible parts of a scallop are the round white muscle and the orange and white coral or roe. The frilly skirt surrounding the muscle – the gills and mantle – may be used for making shellfish stock. All other parts should be discarded.

This dish looks so impressive – the combination of colours making it look almost too good to eat!

Mussels *in* Black Bean Sauce

1 Place the green-lipped mussels in a large bowl, sprinkle with the cumin seeds and toss well to coat. Set aside until required.

2 Heat the vegetable oil in a preheated wok or large, heavy-based frying pan, swirling the oil around the base of the wok until it is very hot.

3 Add the leeks, garlic and red pepper to the wok and stir-fry for 5 minutes, or until the vegetables are tender.

4 Add the bamboo shoots, baby spinach leaves and cooked green-lipped mussels to the wok and stir-fry for about 2 minutes.

5 Pour the black bean sauce over the ingredients in the wok, toss well to coat in the sauce and simmer for a few seconds, stirring occasionally.

6 Transfer the stir-fry to warm serving bowls and serve immediately.

SERVES 4

350 g/12 oz cooked, shelled
  green-lipped mussels
1 tsp cumin seeds
2 tbsp vegetable oil
350 g/12 oz leeks, shredded
2 garlic cloves, crushed
1 red pepper, deseeded and sliced
50 g/1¾ oz canned bamboo shoots, drained
  and rinsed
175 g/6 oz baby spinach leaves
160 g/5¾ oz jar black bean sauce

NUTRITION
Calories *174*; Sugars *4 g*; Protein *19 g*;
Carbohydrate *6 g*; Fat *8 g*; Saturates *1 g*

⭐⭐   easy

🕐   5 mins

🕐   10 mins

 COOK'S TIP

If green-lipped mussels are not available, they can be bought shelled in cans and jars from most large supermarkets.

Oysters are more commonly eaten raw, but are just as delicious when cooked quickly, as in this recipe, and combined with citrus flavours.

Oysters *with* Tofu

SERVES 4

2 tbsp sunflower oil
225 g/8 oz leeks, sliced thinly
350 g/12 oz tofu, cut into bite-sized pieces
350 g/12 oz shelled oysters
2 tbsp fresh lemon juice
1 tsp cornflour
2 tbsp light soy sauce
100 ml/3½ fl oz fish stock
2 tbsp chopped fresh coriander
1 tsp finely grated lemon rind

1 Heat the sunflower oil in a preheated wok or large, heavy-based frying pan. Add the leeks to the wok and stir-fry for about 2 minutes.

2 Add the tofu and oysters to the wok or frying pan and stir-fry for a further 1–2 minutes.

3 Mix together the lemon juice, cornflour, light soy sauce and fish stock in a small bowl, stirring until well blended.

4 Pour the cornflour mixture into the wok and cook, stirring occasionally, until the juices start to thicken.

5 Transfer to serving bowls and scatter the coriander and lemon rind on top. Serve immediately.

NUTRITION
Calories 175; Sugars 2 g; Protein 18 g;
Carbohydrate 3 g; Fat 10 g; Saturates 1 g

easy

5 mins

10 mins

🧑‍🍳 **COOK'S TIP**

Shelled clams or mussels could be used instead of the oysters, if you prefer.

The delicate flavours of Chinese leaves and crab meat are enhanced by the coconut milk in this recipe.

Crab *with* Chinese Leaves

1 Heat the vegetable oil in a preheated wok or large, heavy-based frying pan.

2 Add the mushrooms and garlic to the wok or frying pan and stir-fry for 3 minutes, or until softened.

3 Add the spring onions and Chinese leaves to the wok and stir-fry until the leaves have wilted.

4 Mix together the mild curry paste and coconut milk in a small bowl.

5 Add the mixture to the wok, together with the crab meat and chilli flakes. Mix together until well combined.

6 Heat the mixture in the wok until the juices start to bubble.

7 Transfer the stir-fry to warm serving bowls and serve immediately.

SERVES 4

2 tbsp vegetable oil
225 g/8 oz shiitake mushrooms, sliced
2 garlic cloves, crushed
6 spring onions, sliced
1 head Chinese leaves, shredded
1 tbsp mild curry paste
6 tbsp coconut milk
200 g/7 oz canned white crab meat, drained
1 tsp dried chilli flakes

NUTRITION
Calories *109*; Sugars *1 g*; Protein *11 g*;
Carbohydrate *2 g*; Fat *6 g*; Saturates *1 g*

⭐⭐   easy

🕐   5 mins

🕐   10 mins

 COOK'S TIP

Shiitake mushrooms are now readily available in the fresh vegetable section of most large supermarkets.

Squid is really wonderful if quickly cooked as in this recipe and, contrary to popular belief, it is not tough and rubbery unless it is overcooked.

Squid *with* Black Bean Sauce

SERVES 4

2 tbsp plain flour
½ tsp salt
450 g/1 lb squid rings
2 tbsp groundnut oil
1 green pepper, deseeded and sliced
1 red onion, sliced
160 g/5¾ oz jar black bean sauce

1 Place the plain flour and salt in a bowl and mix together. Add the squid rings and toss until they are evenly coated.

2 Heat the groundnut oil in a large preheated wok or heavy-based frying pan, swirling the oil around the base of the wok until it is really hot.

3 Add the green pepper and red onion to the wok and stir-fry for about 2 minutes, or until the vegetables are just beginning to soften.

4 Add the squid rings to the wok and cook for a further 5 minutes, or until the squid is cooked through. Be careful not to overcook the squid.

5 Add the black bean sauce to the wok and heat through until the juices are bubbling. Transfer the stir-fry to warm serving bowls and serve immediately.

NUTRITION
Calories *180*; Sugars *2 g*; Protein *19 g*;
Carbohydrate *10 g*; Fat *7 g*; Saturates *1 g*

easy

5 mins

8 mins

🍳 **COOK'S TIP**

Serve this recipe with fried rice or noodles, tossed in soy sauce, if you wish.

Squid is a delicious seafood which, if prepared and cooked correctly, is a quick cooking, attractive and tasty ingredient.

Squid *with* Oyster Sauce

1 To prepare the squid, cut down the centre of the body lengthways. Flatten the squid out, inside uppermost, and score a lattice design deep into the flesh, using a sharp knife. Rinse and pat dry the squid with kitchen paper.

2 To make the sauce, combine the oyster sauce, soy sauce, sugar and garlic in a small bowl. Stir to dissolve the sugar and set aside until required.

3 Heat the oil in a preheated wok or large, heavy-based frying pan until almost smoking. Lower the heat slightly, add the squid and stir-fry until they curl up. Remove with a slotted spoon and drain thoroughly on kitchen paper.

4 Pour all but 2 tablespoons of the oil from the wok and return it to the heat. Add the ginger and mangetout and stir-fry for 1 minute.

5 Return the squid to the wok and pour in the sauce and hot fish stock. Leave to simmer for 3 minutes, until thickened. Transfer to a warm serving dish, garnish with pepper triangles and serve immediately.

SERVES 4

450 g/1 lb squid
150 ml/5 fl oz vegetable oil
1 tsp grated fresh root ginger
60 g/2 oz mangetout
5 tbsp hot fish stock
red pepper triangles, to garnish

sauce
1 tbsp oyster sauce
1 tbsp light soy sauce
pinch of caster sugar
1 garlic clove, crushed

NUTRITION
Calories *320*; Sugars *1 g*; Protein *18 g*;
Carbohydrate *2 g*; Fat *26 g*; Saturates *3 g*

⭐⭐⭐   moderate

🕐   5 mins

🕐   10 mins

👨‍🍳 COOK'S TIP

Take care not to overcook the squid, otherwise it will become rubbery.

Vegetables

Vegetables play an important role in wok and stir-fry cooking in the Far East and are used extensively in all meals. It is perfectly possible to enjoy a meal from a selection of the following recipes contained in this chapter without meat or fish. Baby corn cobs, Chinese leaves and green beans, young spinach leaves and pak choi can all bring a unique flavour and freshness to a stir-fried dish. Native Far Eastern people enjoy their vegetables crisp, so cooking times in this chapter reflect this factor in order to bring out the flavours and textures of the ingredients used.

When selecting vegetables for cooking, importance is attached to the freshness of the ingredients used. Always buy firm, crisp vegetables, and cook them as soon as possible after buying. Another point to remember is to wash the vegetables just before cutting and to cook them as soon as they have been cut so that the vitamin content is not lost through evaporation.

WOK & STIR-FRY

Chinese leaves are rather similar to lettuce but have a slightly sweeter flavour and a crisp texture.

Honey-fried Chinese Leaves

SERVES 4

1 tbsp peanut oil
1 tsp grated fresh root ginger
2 garlic cloves, crushed
1 fresh red chilli, sliced
450 g/1 lb Chinese leaves, shredded
1 tbsp Chinese rice wine or dry sherry
4½ tsp light soy sauce
1 tbsp clear honey
125 ml/4 fl oz orange juice
1 tbsp sesame oil
2 tsp sesame seeds
orange rind, to garnish

1 Heat the peanut oil in a preheated wok or large, heavy-based frying pan. Add the ginger, garlic and chilli to the wok and stir-fry for about 30 seconds.

2 Add the Chinese leaves, Chinese rice wine, soy sauce, honey and orange juice to the wok and bring to the boil. Reduce the heat and simmer for 5 minutes.

3 Add the sesame oil to the wok, sprinkle the sesame seeds on top and mix until well combined.

4 Transfer the stir-fry to a warm serving dish, garnish with the orange rind and serve immediately.

NUTRITION

Calories *121*; Sugars *6 g*; Protein *5 g*; Carbohydrate *10 g*; Fat *7 g*; Saturates *1 g*

easy

5 mins

10 mins

🧑‍🍳 COOK'S TIP

Single-flower honey has a more individual flavour than blended honey. Acacia honey is typically Chinese, but you could also try clover, lemon blossom, lime flower or orange blossom.

Warm cucumbers are absolutely delicious, especially when combined with the heat of chilli and the flavour of ginger.

Stir-fried Chilli Cucumber

1 Peel the cucumbers and cut in half lengthways. Scrape the seeds from the centre with a teaspoon or melon baller and discard.

2 Cut the cucumber into strips and place on a plate. Sprinkle the salt over the cucumber strips and set aside for 20 minutes. Rinse well under cold running water and pat dry with kitchen paper.

3 Heat the vegetable oil in a preheated wok or large frying pan until it is almost smoking. Lower the heat slightly and add the garlic, ginger, chillies and spring onions and stir-fry for 30 seconds.

4 Add the cucumbers to the wok, together with the yellow bean sauce and honey and stir-fry for 30 seconds.

5 Add the water and cook over a high heat until most of the water has evaporated and the cucumber is tender.

6 Sprinkle the sesame oil over the stir-fry. Transfer to a warm serving dish and serve immediately.

SERVES 4

2 cucumbers
2 tsp salt
1 tbsp vegetable oil
2 garlic cloves, crushed
1 tsp grated fresh root ginger
2 fresh red chillies, chopped
2 spring onions, chopped
1 tsp yellow bean sauce
1 tbsp clear honey
125 ml/4 fl oz water
1 tsp sesame oil

NUTRITION
Calories 67; Sugars 4 g; Protein 1 g;
Carbohydrate 5 g; Fat 5 g; Saturates 1 g

⭐⭐   easy

🕐   30 mins

🕐   5 mins

👨‍🍳 COOK'S TIP

The cucumber is sprinkled with salt and left to stand in order to draw out the excess water, thus preventing a soggy meal!

These beans are cooked simply in a spicy, hot sauce for a tasty and very easy side dish.

Green Bean Stir-fry

SERVES 4

2 tbsp peanut oil
450 g/1 lb thin green beans, halved
2 fresh red chillies, deseeded and sliced
½ tsp ground star anise
1 garlic clove, crushed
2 tbsp light soy sauce
2 tsp clear honey
½ tsp sesame oil

1 Heat the oil in a preheated wok or large, heavy-based frying pan until it is almost smoking.

2 Lower the heat slightly, add the green beans and stir-fry for 1 minute.

3 Add the red chillies, star anise and garlic to the wok and stir-fry for a further 30 seconds.

4 Mix together the soy sauce, honey and sesame oil in a small bowl.

5 Stir the sauce mixture into the wok. Cook for 2 minutes, tossing the beans to ensure that they are thoroughly coated in the sauce.

6 Transfer the mixture to a warm serving dish and serve immediately.

NUTRITION
Calories 86; Sugars 4 g; Protein 2 g;
Carbohydrate 6 g; Fat 6 g; Saturates 1 g

easy

5 mins

5 mins

COOK'S TIP

This recipe is surprisingly delicious made with Brussels sprouts instead of green beans. Trim the sprouts, then shred them finely. Stir-fry the sprouts in hot oil for 2 minutes, then proceed with the recipe from step 2.

Ginger and broccoli are a perfect combination of flavours and make an exceptionally tasty side dish.

Gingered Broccoli

1 Heat the peanut oil in a preheated wok or large, heavy-based frying pan. Add the garlic and ginger and stir-fry for 30 seconds.

2 Add the broccoli, leek and water chestnuts and stir-fry for 3–4 minutes.

3 Add the caster sugar, vegetable stock and dark soy sauce to the wok, reduce the heat and simmer for 4–5 minutes, or until the broccoli is almost cooked.

4 Blend the cornflour with the water to form a smooth paste and stir it into the wok. Bring to the boil and cook, stirring constantly, for 1 minute, or until thickened. (If using large strips of ginger, remove from the wok and discard.)

5 Transfer the vegetables to a serving dish and serve immediately.

SERVES 4

2 tbsp peanut oil
1 garlic clove, crushed
5-cm/2-inch piece fresh root ginger, chopped or shredded finely
675 g/1½ lb broccoli florets
1 leek, sliced
75 g/2¾ oz water chestnuts, drained and halved
½ tsp caster sugar
125 ml/4 fl oz vegetable stock
1 tsp dark soy sauce
1 tsp cornflour
2 tsp water

NUTRITION
Calories *118*; Sugars *3 g*; Protein *8 g*; Carbohydrate *6 g*; Fat *7 g*; Saturates *1 g*

⭐⭐ easy
🕐 5 mins
🕐 15 mins

🍳 **COOK'S TIP**

Use spinach instead of the broccoli. Cut the stalks into 5-cm/2-inch lengths, keeping the leaves separate. Add the stalks with the leek in step 2 and add the leaves 2 minutes later. Reduce the cooking time in step 3 to 3–4 minutes.

The green lentils used in this recipe require soaking but it's worth the time for the flavour. If time is short, use red split lentils that don't need soaking.

Green Lentil Pan-fry

SERVES 4

150 g/5½ oz dried green lentils
4 tbsp butter or vegetarian margarine
2 garlic cloves, crushed
2 tbsp olive oil
1 tbsp cider vinegar
1 red onion, cut into 8 pieces
50 g/1¾ oz baby corn cobs, halved
   lengthways
1 yellow pepper, deseeded and cut into strips
1 red pepper, deseeded and cut into strips
50 g/1¾ oz green beans, halved
125 ml/4 fl oz vegetable stock
2 tbsp honey
salt and pepper
crusty bread, to serve

1 Soak the lentils in a large saucepan of cold water for 25 minutes. Bring to the boil, reduce the heat and simmer for 20 minutes. Drain thoroughly.

2 Add 1 tablespoon of the butter, 1 garlic clove, 1 tablespoon of oil and the vinegar to the lentils and mix well.

3 Add the remaining butter and oil to a preheated wok or large, heavy-based frying pan and when hot add the remaining garlic, the onion, corn cobs, peppers and green beans and stir-fry for 3–4 minutes.

4 Add the vegetable stock and bring to the boil. Cook the mixture for about 10 minutes, or until the liquid has evaporated.

5 Add the honey and season with salt and pepper to taste. Stir in the lentil mixture and cook for 1 minute to heat through. Spoon on to warmed serving plates and serve with crusty bread.

NUTRITION
Calories *490*; Sugars *12 g*; Protein *26 g*;
Carbohydrates *61 g*; Fat *18 g*; Saturates *8 g*

⭐⭐   easy
🕐   30 mins
🕐   45 mins

 COOK'S TIP

This stir-fry is very versatile – you can use a mixture of any of your favourite vegetables, if you prefer, such as courgettes, carrots and mangetout.

In this recipe, spinach is fried with spices and then braised in a soy-flavoured sauce with bamboo shoots for a rich, delicious dish.

Bamboo *with* Spinach

1 Heat the peanut oil in a preheated wok or large, heavy-based frying pan, swirling the oil around the base of the wok until it is very hot.

2 Add the spinach and bamboo shoots to the wok and stir-fry for 1 minute.

3 Add the garlic, chillies and cinnamon to the mixture in the wok and stir-fry for a further 30 seconds.

4 Stir in the stock, sugar, salt and light soy sauce, cover and cook over a medium heat for 5 minutes, or until the vegetables are cooked through and the sauce has reduced. (If there is too much cooking liquid, blend a little cornflour with double the quantity of cold water and stir it into the sauce.)

5 Transfer the bamboo shoots and spinach to a serving dish and serve.

SERVES 4

3 tbsp peanut oil
225 g/8 oz spinach, chopped
175 g/6 oz canned bamboo shoots, drained and rinsed
1 garlic clove, crushed
2 fresh red chillies, sliced
pinch of ground cinnamon
300 ml/10 fl oz vegetable stock
pinch of sugar
pinch of salt
1 tbsp light soy sauce

NUTRITION
Calories *105*; Sugars *1 g*; Protein *3 g*; Carbohydrate *3 g*; Fat *9 g*; Saturates *2 g*

⭐⭐ easy
🕐 5 mins
🕐 10 mins

👨‍🍳 COOK'S TIP

Fresh bamboo shoots are rarely available in the West. Canned bamboo shoots are quite satisfactory, as they are used to provide a crunchy texture, rather than for their flavour, which is quite bland.

Dim sum are small Chinese parcels, which may be filled with a variety of delicious fillings, and are then steamed or fried and served with a dipping sauce.

Vegetable Dim Sum

SERVES 4

2 spring onions, chopped
25 g/1 oz green beans, chopped
½ small carrot, chopped finely
1 fresh red chilli, chopped
25 g/1 oz beansprouts, chopped
25 g/1 oz button mushrooms, chopped
25 g/1 oz unsalted cashew nuts, chopped
1 small egg, beaten
2 tbsp cornflour
1 tsp light soy sauce
1 tsp hoisin sauce
1 tsp sesame oil
32 wonton wrappers
oil, for deep-frying
1 tbsp sesame seeds
soy or plum sauce, for dipping

1 Mix all of the vegetables together in a bowl. Add the nuts, egg, cornflour, soy sauce, hoisin sauce and sesame oil to the bowl. Mix well.

2 Lay the wonton wrappers out on a chopping board and spoon small quantities of the mixture into the centre of each. Gather the wrapper around the filling to make little parcels, leaving the top open.

3 Heat the oil for deep-frying in a wok or large, heavy-based saucepan to 180°C/350°F, or until a cube of bread browns in 30 seconds. Fry the wontons, in batches, for 1–2 minutes, or until golden brown. Drain on kitchen paper and keep warm while frying the remaining wontons.

4 Sprinkle the sesame seeds over the wontons. Serve the vegetable dim sum with a soy or plum dipping sauce.

NUTRITION
Calories 295; Sugars 1 g; Protein 5 g;
Carbohydrate 20 g; Fat 22 g; Saturates 6 g

moderate

15 mins

15 mins

🍳 COOK'S TIP

If preferred, arrange the wontons on a heatproof plate and then cook in a steamer for 5–7 minutes for a healthier alternative.

The Chinese are known for their colourful, crisp vegetables, quickly stir-fried. In this recipe, they are tossed in a tasty soy and hoisin sauce.

Chinese Fried Vegetables

1 Heat the peanut oil in a preheated wok or large, heavy-based frying pan until it is almost smoking.

2 Add the broccoli florets, ginger, onions and celery to the wok and stir-fry for 1 minute.

3 Add the spinach, mangetout, spring onions and garlic and stir-fry for a further 3–4 minutes.

4 Mix together the soy sauce, caster sugar, sherry, hoisin sauce and vegetable stock in a small bowl.

5 Pour the stock mixture into the wok, mixing well to coat the vegetables.

6 Cover the wok and cook over a medium heat for 2–3 minutes, or until the vegetables are cooked through, but still crisp.

7 Transfer the vegetables to a warm serving dish and serve immediately.

SERVES 4

2 tbsp peanut oil
350 g/12 oz broccoli florets
1 tbsp chopped fresh root ginger
2 onions, cut into 8 pieces
3 celery sticks, sliced
175 g/6 oz baby spinach
125 g/4½ oz mangetout
6 spring onions, quartered
2 garlic cloves, crushed
2 tbsp light soy sauce
2 tsp caster sugar
2 tbsp dry sherry
1 tbsp hoisin sauce
150 ml/5 fl oz vegetable stock

NUTRITION
Calories *137*; Sugars *7 g*; Protein *8 g*;
Carbohydrate *10 g*; Fat *7 g*; Saturates *11 g*

⭐⭐   easy

🕐   5 mins

🕐   10 mins

👒 COOK'S TIP

You can use this mixture to fill Chinese pancakes. They are available from Chinese food stores and can be reheated in a steamer in 2-3 minutes.

A mixture of mushrooms, commonly used in Western cooking, have been used in this recipe for a richly flavoured dish.

Spicy Mushrooms

SERVES 4

2 tbsp peanut oil
2 garlic cloves, crushed
3 spring onions, chopped
300 g/10½ oz button mushrooms
2 large open-cap mushrooms, sliced
125 g/4½ oz oyster mushrooms
1 tsp chilli sauce
1 tbsp dark soy sauce
1 tbsp hoisin sauce
1 tbsp wine vinegar
½ tsp ground Szechuan pepper
1 tbsp dark brown sugar
1 tsp sesame oil
chopped fresh parsley, to garnish

1 Heat the peanut oil in a preheated wok or large, heavy-based frying pan until almost smoking.

2 Reduce the heat slightly, add the garlic and spring onions to the wok and stir-fry for 30 seconds.

3 Add all the mushrooms to the wok with the chilli sauce, dark soy sauce, hoisin sauce, wine vinegar, ground Szechuan pepper and dark brown sugar and stir-fry for 4–5 minutes, or until the mushrooms have softened. Stir constantly to prevent the mixture sticking.

4 Sprinkle the sesame oil over the mixture in the wok. Transfer to a warm serving dish, garnish with parsley and serve immediately.

NUTRITION
Calories 103; Sugars 4 g; Protein 3 g; Carbohydrate 5 g; Fat 8 g; Saturates 2 g

⭐⭐ easy
🕐 5 mins
🕐 10 mins

 COOK'S TIP

If Chinese dried mushrooms are available, add a small quantity to this dish. Wood ears are widely available dried from Chinese food stores. They should be rinsed, soaked in warm water for 20 minutes and rinsed again before use.

Tofu is available in different forms from both Chinese and Western supermarkets. The block form of tofu is used here.

Fried Tofu *and* Vegetables

1 Heat the oil in a preheated wok or large, heavy-based frying pan until almost smoking. Reduce the heat, add the tofu and stir-fry until golden brown. Remove from the wok with a slotted spoon and drain on kitchen paper.

2 Pour all but 2 tablespoons of the oil from the wok and return it to the heat. Add the leek, corn cobs, mangetout, red pepper and bamboo shoots, then stir-fry for 2–3 minutes.

3 Add the Chinese rice wine, oyster sauce, soy sauce, sugar, salt and stock to the wok and bring to the boil. Blend the cornflour with the water to form a smooth paste and stir it into the sauce. Return the sauce to the boil and cook, stirring constantly, until thickened and clear.

4 Stir the cooked tofu into the mixture in the wok and cook for about 1 minute, until hot. Serve immediately.

SERVES 4

150 ml/5 fl oz vegetable oil
450 g/1 lb tofu, cut into
   2.5-cm/1-inch cubes
1 leek, sliced
4 baby corn cobs, halved lengthways
55 g/2 oz mangetout
1 red pepper, deseeded and diced
55 g/2 oz canned bamboo shoots, drained
1 tbsp Chinese rice wine or dry sherry
4 tbsp oyster sauce
3 tsp light soy sauce
2 tsp caster sugar
salt
50 ml/2 fl oz vegetable stock
1 tsp cornflour
2 tsp water

NUTRITION
Calories 367; Sugars 5 g; Protein 13 g; Carbohydrate 11 g; Fat 30 g; Saturates 4 g

⭐⭐ easy
🕙 10 mins
🕐 15 mins

🅦 COOK'S TIP

Tofu is relatively bland, but it readily absorbs stronger flavours.

Vegan *and* Vegetarian

As vegetables are so plentiful and diverse in the Far East, they play a major role in the diet. Other ingredients, such as tofu and quorn, are also added to the vegetarian diet, which is both a healthy and an economical choice. Tofu is produced from the soya bean, which is grown in abundance in these countries. The cake variety of tofu is frequently used in stir-frying for texture and it is perfect for absorbing all of the component flavours of the dish. It is also an ideal ingredient for the vegan cook.

The wok is perfect for cooking vegetables as it cooks them very quickly, which helps to retain their nutrients and crispness. This produces a range of colourful and flavoursome recipes, which display the wonderful versatility of vegetables.

This sweet and spicy dish is flavoured with mango chutney and red chillies for a really wonderful combination of flavours.

Spiced Aubergine

SERVES 4

3 tbsp groundnut oil
2 onions, sliced
2 garlic cloves, chopped
2 aubergines, diced
2 fresh red chillies, deseeded and
    finely chopped
2 tbsp demerara sugar
6 spring onions, sliced
3 tbsp mango chutney
oil, for deep-frying
2 garlic cloves, sliced, to garnish

1 Heat the groundnut oil in a large preheated wok or large, heavy-based frying pan, swirling the oil around the base of the wok until it is really hot.

2 Add the onions and chopped garlic to the wok, stirring well.

3 Add the aubergines and chillies to the wok and stir-fry for 5 minutes.

4 Add the demerara sugar, spring onions and mango chutney to the wok, stirring well, and bring to the boil.

5 Reduce the heat, cover and leave to simmer, stirring from time to time, for 15 minutes until the aubergine is tender.

6 Transfer the stir-fry to serving bowls and keep warm.

7 Heat the oil for deep-frying in the wok and quickly stir-fry the slices of garlic, until they brown slightly. Garnish the stir-fry with the deep-fried garlic and serve immediately.

NUTRITION
Calories 208; Sugars 17 g; Protein 1 g;
Carbohydrate 17 g; Fat 15 g; Saturates 2 g

easy

5 mins

25 mins

🍽 COOK'S TIP

Chillies vary enormously in their level of heat so always use with caution. As a general guide, the smaller the chilli, the hotter it will be. The seeds are the hottest part and so are usually discarded for a milder flavour.

These small corn balls have a wonderful hot and sweet flavour, offset by the aromatic coriander.

Deep-fried Chilli Corn Balls

1 In a large bowl, mix together the spring onions, coriander, sweetcorn, chilli powder, chilli sauce, coconut, egg and polenta until well blended.

2 Cover the bowl with clingfilm and leave to stand for about 10 minutes.

3 Heat the oil for deep-frying in a large preheated wok or large, heavy-based saucepan to 180°C/350°F or until a cube of bread browns in 30 seconds.

4 Carefully drop spoonfuls of the chilli and polenta mixture into the hot oil. Deep-fry the chilli corn balls, in batches, for 4–5 minutes, or until crispy and a deep golden brown colour.

5 Remove the chilli corn balls with a slotted spoon, transfer to kitchen paper and leave to drain thoroughly.

6 Transfer the chilli corn balls to serving plates and serve with sweet chilli dipping sauce.

SERVES 4

6 spring onions, sliced
3 tbsp chopped fresh coriander
225 g/8 oz canned sweetcorn
    kernels, drained
1 tsp mild chilli powder
1 tbsp sweet chilli sauce
25 g/1 oz dessicated coconut
1 egg
75 g/2¾ oz polenta
oil, for deep-frying
sweet chilli sauce, to serve

NUTRITION
Calories 248; Sugars 6 g; Protein 6 g; Carbohydrate 30 g; Fat 12 g; Saturates 5 g

easy

15 mins

30 mins

🍳 COOK'S TIP

For safe deep-frying in a round-bottomed wok, place it on a wok rack so that it rests securely. Only half-fill the wok with oil. Never leave the wok unattended over a high heat.

Butternut squash is, as its name suggests, deliciously buttery and nutty in flavour. If squash is not in season, use sweet potatoes instead.

Butternut Squash Stir-fry

SERVES 4

3 tbsp groundnut oil
1 kg/2 lb 4 oz butternut squash, deseeded, peeled and cubed
1 onion, sliced
2 garlic cloves, crushed
1 tsp coriander seeds
1 tsp cumin seeds
2 tbsp chopped fresh coriander
150 ml/5 fl oz coconut milk
100 ml/3½ fl oz water
100 g/3½ oz salted cashew nuts

to garnish
freshly grated lime rind
chopped fresh coriander
lime wedges

1 Heat the groundnut oil in a preheated wok or large, heavy-based frying pan.

2 Add the butternut squash, onion and garlic and stir-fry for 5 minutes.

3 Stir in the coriander seeds, cumin seeds and fresh coriander and stir-fry for 1 minute.

4 Add the coconut milk and water to the wok and bring to the boil. Reduce the heat, cover and simmer for 10–15 minutes, or until the squash is tender.

5 Add the cashew nuts and stir to combine.

6 Transfer to warm serving dishes and garnish with freshly grated lime rind, fresh coriander and lime wedges. Serve hot immediately.

NUTRITION
Calories *301*; Sugars *4 g*; Protein *9 g*; Carbohydrate *19 g*; Fat *22 g*; Saturates *4 g*

⭐⭐ easy
🕐 5 mins
🕐 25 mins

 COOK'S TIP

If you do not have coconut milk, grate some creamed coconut into the dish with the water in step 4.

This is a simple side dish, which is an ideal accompaniment to main vegetarian dishes.

Leeks *with* Yellow Bean Sauce

1 Heat the groundnut oil in a preheated wok or large, heavy-based frying pan until smoking.

2 Add the leeks, Chinese leaves and baby corn cobs to the wok.

3 Stir-fry the vegetables over a high heat for about 5 minutes, or until the edges of the vegetables are slightly brown.

4 Add the spring onions to the wok, stirring to combine.

5 Add the yellow bean sauce to the wok. Stir-fry the mixture for a further 2 minutes, or until heated through and the vegetables are thoroughly coated in the sauce.

6 Transfer the vegetables and sauce to warm serving dishes and serve.

SERVES 4

3 tbsp groundnut oil
450 g/1 lb leeks, thinly sliced
225 g/8 oz Chinese leaves, shredded
175 g/6 oz baby corn cobs, halved
    lengthways
6 spring onions, sliced diagonally
4 tbsp yellow bean sauce

NUTRITION
Calories *131*; Sugars *3 g*; Protein *6 g*;
Carbohydrate *7 g*; Fat *9 g*; Saturates *2 g*

⭐⭐   easy
🕑   5 mins
🕐   10 mins

🍴 COOK'S TIP

Yellow bean sauce adds an authentic Chinese flavour to stir-fries. It is made from crushed, salted soya beans mixed with flour and spices to make a thick paste. It is mild in flavour and is excellent with a range of vegetables.

Plum sauce is readily available in jars and has a terrific, sweet flavour, which complements most types of vegetable.

Pak Choi *with* Cashew Nuts

SERVES 4

2 tbsp groundnut oil
2 red onions, cut into thin wedges
175 g/6 oz red cabbage, shredded thinly
225 g/8 oz pak choi, leaves separated
2 tbsp plum sauce
100 g/3½ oz roasted cashew nuts

1 Heat the groundnut oil in a preheated wok or large, heavy-based frying pan until the oil is really hot.

2 Add the onion wedges to the wok and stir-fry for about 5 minutes, or until the onions just begin to brown.

3 Add the red cabbage to the wok and stir-fry for a further 2–3 minutes.

4 Add the pak choi leaves to the wok and stir-fry for about 5 minutes, or until the leaves have just wilted.

5 Drizzle the plum sauce over the vegetables, toss together until well combined and heat until the liquid is bubbling.

6 Scatter with the roasted cashew nuts and transfer to warm serving bowls.

NUTRITION

Calories *241*; Sugars *7 g*; Protein *7 g*;
Carbohydrate *11 g*; Fat *19 g*; Saturates *4 g*

⭐ very easy

🕐 5 mins

🕐 15 mins

👨‍🍳 COOK'S TIP

Use unsalted peanuts instead of the cashew nuts, if you prefer.

These courgette fritters are irresistible and could be served as a starter or snack with a chilli dip.

Deep-fried Courgettes

1 Lightly whip the egg white in a small bowl until foamy.

2 Mix the cornflour, salt and Chinese five-spice powder together and sprinkle on to a large plate.

3 Heat the oil for deep-frying in a large preheated wok or large, heavy-based saucepan.

4 Dip each piece of courgette into the beaten egg white, then coat in the cornflour and five-spice mixture.

5 Deep-fry the courgettes, in batches, for about 5 minutes, or until pale golden and crispy. Repeat this process with the remaining courgettes.

6 Remove the courgettes with a slotted spoon and leave to drain on kitchen paper while deep-frying the remainder.

7 Transfer the courgettes to serving plates and serve with the chilli dip.

SERVES 4

1 egg white
50 g/1¾ oz cornflour
1 tsp salt
1 tsp Chinese five-spice powder
oil, for deep-frying
450 g/1 lb courgettes, sliced into sticks or rounds
chilli dip, to serve

NUTRITION
Calories 117; Sugars 2 g; Protein 3 g; Carbohydrate 14 g; Fat 6 g; Saturates 1 g

⭐ very easy

🕐 5 mins

🕐 20 mins

👑 COOK'S TIP

Alter the seasoning by using chilli powder or curry powder instead of the Chinese five-spice powder, if you prefer.

This stir-fry is the perfect accompaniment to tofu dishes, and it is so quick and simple to make.

Honey-fried Spinach

SERVES 4

3 tbsp groundnut oil
350 g/12 oz shiitake mushrooms, sliced
2 garlic cloves, crushed
350 g/12 oz baby spinach leaves
2 tbsp dry sherry
2 tbsp clear honey
4 spring onions, sliced

1 Heat the groundnut oil in a preheated wok or large, heavy-based frying pan.

2 Add the shiitake mushrooms to the wok and stir-fry for about 5 minutes, or until the mushrooms have softened.

3 Add the garlic and spinach to the wok and stir-fry for a further 2–3 minutes, or until the spinach leaves have wilted.

4 Mix together the dry sherry and clear honey in a small bowl until well combined. Drizzle the sherry and honey mixture over the spinach and heat through, stirring to coat the spinach leaves thoroughly in the mixture.

5 Transfer the stir-fry to warm serving dishes, scatter with the spring onions and serve immediately.

NUTRITION
Calories *146*; Sugars *9 g*; Protein *4 g*; Carbohydrate *10 g*; Fat *9 g*; Saturates *2 g*

easy

5 mins

15 mins

COOK'S TIP

Single-flower honey has a more individual flavour than blended honey. Acacia honey is typically Chinese, but you could also try clover, lemon blossom, lime flower or orange blossom honey.

Although sweet and sour flavourings are mainly associated with pork, they are ideal for adding interest to vegetables as in this tasty recipe.

Sweet *and* Sour Cauliflower

1 Bring a large saucepan of water to the boil. Add the cauliflower to the pan and cook for 2 minutes. Drain the cauliflower thoroughly.

2 Heat the sunflower oil in a preheated wok or large, heavy-based frying pan.

3 Add the onion and carrots to the wok and stir-fry for about 5 minutes.

4 Add the cauliflower and mangetout to the wok and stir-fry for 2–3 minutes.

5 Add the mango and beansprouts to the wok and stir-fry for 2 minutes.

6 Mix together the coriander, lime juice, honey and coconut milk in a bowl.

7 Add the coriander and coconut mixture to the wok and stir-fry for about 2 minutes. or until the juices are bubbling.

8 Transfer the cauliflower stir-fry to serving dishes and serve immediately.

SERVES 4

450 g/1 lb cauliflower florets
2 tbsp sunflower oil
1 onion, sliced
225 g/8 oz carrots, sliced
100 g/3½ oz mangetout
1 ripe mango, peeled, stoned and sliced
100 g/3½ oz beansprouts
3 tbsp chopped fresh coriander
3 tbsp fresh lime juice
1 tbsp clear honey
6 tbsp coconut milk

NUTRITION
Calories *154*; Sugars *16 g*; Protein *6 g*;
Carbohydrate *17 g*; Fat *7 g*; Saturates *1 g*

⭐⭐   easy
🕐   5 mins
🕐   15 mins

 COOK'S TIP

You could use broccoli instead of cauliflower, if preferred.

This quick dish is an ideal lunchtime meal, packed with mixed mushrooms in a flavoursome sweet sauce.

Stir-fried Japanese Noodles

SERVES 4

250 g/9 oz Japanese egg noodles
2 tbsp sunflower oil
1 red onion, sliced
1 garlic clove, crushed
450 g/1 lb mixed mushrooms, such as shiitake, oyster or brown cap
350 g/12 oz pak choi or Chinese leaves, leaves separated
2 tbsp sweet sherry
6 tbsp oyster sauce
4 spring onions, sliced
1 tbsp toasted sesame seeds

1 Place the Japanese egg noodles in a large bowl. Pour enough boiling water over to cover and leave to soak for 10 minutes.

2 Heat the sunflower oil in a preheated wok or large, heavy-based frying pan.

3 Add the red onion and garlic to the wok and stir-fry for 2–3 minutes, or until softened.

4 Add the mushrooms to the wok and stir-fry for about 5 minutes, or until they have softened.

5 Drain the egg noodles thoroughly.

6 Add the the pak choi leaves, noodles, sweet sherry and oyster sauce to the wok. Toss all of the ingredients together and stir-fry for 2–3 minutes, or until the liquid is just bubbling.

7 Transfer the mushroom noodles to warm serving bowls and scatter with sliced spring onions and toasted sesame seeds. Serve immediately.

NUTRITION
Calories 379; Sugars 8 g; Protein 12 g; Carbohydrate 53 g; Fat 13 g; Saturates 3 g

easy
15 mins
15 mins

🍲 COOK'S TIP

The variety of mushrooms in supermarkets has greatly improved and a good mixture should be easily obtainable. If not, use the more common button and flat mushrooms.

Although mild in flavour, tofu will absorb the other flavours in this dish. If marinated tofu is used, it will also add a flavour of its own.

Tofu Casserole

1 Heat the peanut oil in a preheated wok or large, heavy-based frying pan.

2 Add the spring onions, celery, broccoli, courgettes, garlic, spinach and tofu to the wok and stir-fry for 3–4 minutes.

3 To make the sauce, mix together the vegetable stock, soy sauce, hoisin sauce, chilli powder and sesame oil in a small flameproof casserole and bring to the boil.

4 Add the stir-fried vegetables and tofu to the casserole, reduce the heat, then cover and simmer for 10 minutes.

5 Transfer the tofu and vegetables to a warm serving dish and serve with rice.

SERVES 4

2 tbsp peanut oil
8 spring onions, cut into batons
2 celery sticks, sliced
125 g/4½ oz broccoli florets
125 g/4½ oz courgettes, sliced
2 garlic cloves, sliced thinly
450 g/1 lb baby spinach leaves
450 g/1 lb tofu, cut into 2.5-cm/
    1-inch cubes
boiled rice, to serve

sauce
425 ml/15 fl oz vegetable stock
2 tbsp light soy sauce
3 tbsp hoisin sauce
½ tsp chilli powder
1 tbsp sesame oil

NUTRITION
Calories *228*; Sugars *3 g*; Protein *16 g*;
Carbohydrate *7 g*; Fat *15 g*; Saturates *2 g*

★★   easy

🕐   5 mins

🕐   15 mins

 COOK'S TIP

This recipe incorporates mainly green vegetables, but you could alter them according to likes and dislikes. Add mushrooms, carrots, baby corn or Chinese leaves, if preferred.

Sweet-and-sour was one of the first Chinese sauces introduced to the West, and still remains one of the most popular.

Sweet *and* Sour Tofu

SERVES 4

2 tbsp vegetable oil
2 garlic cloves, crushed
2 celery sticks, sliced thinly
1 carrot, cut into thin strips
1 green pepper, deseeded and diced
75 g/2³⁄₄ oz mangetout, halved diagonally
8 baby corn cobs
125 g/4¹⁄₂ oz beansprouts
450 g/1 lb tofu, cubed
boiled rice or noodles, to serve

sauce

2 tbsp light brown sugar
2 tbsp rice wine vinegar
225 ml/8 fl oz vegetable stock
1 tsp tomato purée
1 tbsp cornflour

1 Heat the vegetable oil in a preheated wok or large heavy-based frying pan until it is almost smoking. Reduce the heat slightly, add the garlic, celery, carrot, pepper, mangetout and corn cobs and stir-fry for 3–4 minutes.

2 Add the beansprouts and tofu to the wok and cook for 2 minutes, stirring gently, but thoroughly.

3 To make the sauce, combine the sugar, wine vinegar, stock, tomato purée and cornflour, stirring well to mix. Add to the wok, bring to the boil and cook, stirring, until the sauce thickens and clears. Continue to cook for 1 minute. Serve the tofu with rice or noodles.

NUTRITION
Calories *205*; Sugars *12 g*; Protein *11 g*;
Carbohydrate *17 g*; Fat *11 g*; Saturates *1 g*

easy

5 mins

10 mins

🍴 **COOK'S TIP**

Be careful not to break up the fragile cubes of tofu when stirring.

This tasty rice dish can either be served as a main meal or as an accompaniment to other vegetable recipes.

Chinese Vegetable Rice

1 Place the rice and turmeric in a saucepan of lightly salted water and bring to the boil. Reduce the heat and leave to simmer until the rice is just tender. Drain the rice thoroughly. Set aside until required.

2 Heat the sunflower oil in a preheated wok or large, heavy-based frying pan.

3 Add the courgettes to the wok and stir-fry for about 2 minutes.

4 Add the red and green peppers and chilli to the wok and stir-fry for 2–3 minutes.

5 Add the cooked rice to the mixture in the wok, a little at a time, tossing well after each addition.

6 Add the carrot, beansprouts and spring onions to the wok and stir-fry for a further 2 minutes.

7 Drizzle the soy sauce over the stir-fry and serve at once, garnished with extra spring onions, if desired.

SERVES 4

350 g/12 oz long-grain white rice
1 tsp turmeric
2 tbsp sunflower oil
225 g/8 oz courgettes, sliced
1 red pepper, deseeded and sliced
1 green pepper, deseeded and sliced
1 fresh green chilli, deseeded and chopped finely
1 carrot, grated roughly
150 g/5½ oz beansprouts
6 spring onions, sliced, plus extra to garnish (optional)
2 tbsp soy sauce
salt

NUTRITION
Calories *140*; Sugars *3 g*; Protein *3 g*; Carbohydrate *20 g*; Fat *17 g*, Saturates *1 g*

moderate

5 mins

25 mins

COOK'S TIP

For real luxury, add a few saffron strands infused in boiling water instead of the turmeric.

This spicy vegetable stir-fry has rice added to it and can be served as a main meal in itself.

Vegetables *with* Hoisin

SERVES 4

2 tbsp sunflower oil
1 red onion, sliced thinly
100 g/3½ oz carrots, sliced thinly
1 yellow pepper, deseeded and diced
50 g/1¾ oz cooked brown rice
175 g/6 oz mangetout
175 g/6 oz beansprouts
4 tbsp hoisin sauce
1 tbsp snipped fresh chives

1 Heat the sunflower oil in a preheated wok or large, heavy-based frying pan.

2 Add the red onion, carrots and yellow pepper to the wok and stir-fry for about 3 minutes.

3 Add the cooked brown rice, mangetout and beansprouts to the mixture in the wok and stir-fry for a further 2 minutes. Stir briskly to ensure that the ingredients are well mixed and the rice grains are separated.

4 Stir the hoisin sauce into the vegetables and mix until well combined and completely heated through.

5 Transfer the vegetable stir-fry to warm serving dishes and scatter with the snipped fresh chives. Serve immediately.

NUTRITION
Calories *120*; Sugars *6 g*; Protein *4 g*;
Carbohydrate *12 g*; Fat *6 g*; Saturates *1 g*

easy

10 mins

10 mins

🍳 **COOK'S TIP**

Hoisin sauce is a dark brown, reddish sauce made from soy beans, garlic, chilli and various other spices, and is commonly used in Chinese cookery. It may also be used as a dipping sauce.

This is a crunchy and colourful stir-fry, topped with crisp, shredded leeks for both flavour and colour.

Peppers and Chestnuts

1 Heat the oil for deep-frying in a preheated wok or large, heavy-based saucepan.

2 Add the leeks to the wok and fry for 2–3 minutes, or until crispy. Remove from the pan with a slotted spoon and drain on kitchen paper. Set aside until the leeks are required.

3 Pour all but 3 tablespoons of the oil from the wok. Add the yellow, green and red peppers to the wok and stir-fry over a high heat for about 5 minutes, or until they begin to brown at the edges and have softened.

4 Add the water chestnuts, garlic and light soy sauce to the wok and stir-fry the vegetables for a further 2–3 minutes.

5 Spoon the pepper stir-fry on to warm serving plates, sprinkle with the crispy leeks and serve.

SERVES 4

oil, for deep-frying
225 g/8 oz leeks, shredded thinly
1 yellow pepper, deseeded and diced
1 green pepper, deseeded and diced
1 red pepper, deseeded and diced
200 g/7 oz canned water chestnuts, drained and sliced
2 garlic cloves, crushed
3 tbsp light soy sauce

NUTRITION
Calories *192*; Sugars *5 g*; Protein *3 g*; Carbohydrate *13 g*; Fat *14 g*; Saturates *13 g*

⭐⭐ easy
🕐 5 mins
🕐 15 mins

🧑‍🍳 **COOK'S TIP**

Add 1 tablespoon of hoisin sauce with the soy sauce in step 4 for a richer flavour and spice.

Known as Gado Gado in Indonesia, this is a true classic which never fades in popularity. A delicious warm salad, topped with quarters of hard-boiled egg, served with a peanut sauce.

Vegetable Stir-fry *with* Eggs

SERVES 4

2 eggs
2 tbsp vegetable oil
225 g/8 oz carrots, grated coarsely
350 g/12 oz white cabbage, shredded finely
1 red pepper, deseeded and sliced thinly
150 g/5½ oz beansprouts
1 tbsp tomato ketchup
2 tbsp soy sauce
75 g/2¾ oz salted peanuts, chopped
peanut sauce, to serve

1 Bring a small saucepan of water to the boil. Add the eggs to the pan and cook for about 7 minutes. Remove the eggs from the pan and cool under cold running water for 1 minute. Peel the eggs and then cut into quarters.

2 Heat the vegetable oil in a preheated wok or large, heavy-based frying pan.

3 Add the carrots, white cabbage and red pepper to the wok and stir-fry for 3 minutes.

4 Add the beansprouts to the wok and stir-fry for 2 minutes.

5 Mix together the tomato ketchup and soy sauce in a small bowl and add to the wok, stirring well to combine.

6 Add the chopped peanuts to the wok and stir-fry for 1 minute.

7 Transfer the stir-fry to warm serving plates and garnish with the hard-boiled egg quarters. Serve with a peanut sauce.

NUTRITION
Calories *269*; Sugars *12 g*; Protein *12 g*; Carbohydrate *14 g*; Fat *19 g*; Saturates *3 g*

easy

10 mins

15 mins

🍳 COOK'S TIP

The eggs are cooled in cold water after cooking in order to prevent the egg yolk turning black around the edges.

This recipe, as the title suggests, is a colourful mixture of eight vegetables, cooked in a black bean and soy sauce.

Eight Jewel Vegetables

1 Heat the peanut oil in a preheated wok or large, heavy-based frying pan until it is almost smoking.

2 Lower the heat slightly, add the spring onions and garlic and stir-fry for about 30 seconds.

3 Add the green and red peppers, red chilli, water chestnuts and courgette to the wok and stir-fry for 2–3 minutes, or until the vegetables are just beginning to soften.

4 Add the oyster mushrooms, black bean sauce, Chinese rice wine, dark soy sauce, dark brown sugar and water to the wok and stir-fry for a further 4 minutes.

5 Sprinkle the stir-fry with sesame oil and serve immediately.

SERVES 4

2 tbsp peanut oil
6 spring onions, sliced
3 garlic cloves, crushed
1 green pepper, deseeded and diced
1 red pepper, deseeded and diced
1 fresh red chilli, sliced
2 tbsp chopped water chestnuts
1 courgette, chopped
125 g/4½ oz oyster mushrooms
3 tbsp black bean sauce
2 tsp Chinese rice wine or dry sherry
4 tbsp dark soy sauce
1 tsp dark brown sugar
2 tbsp water
1 tsp sesame oil

NUTRITION
Calories 110; Sugars 3 g; Protein 4 g;
Carbohydrate 7 g, Fat 8 g, Saturates 1 g

⭐⭐ easy

🕐 5 mins

🕐 10 mins

🍳 **COOK'S TIP**

Eight jewels or treasures form a traditional part of the Chinese New Year celebrations. The Kitchen God, an important figure, is sent to give a report to heaven, returning on New Year's Eve in time for the feasting.

Marinated tofu is ideal in this recipe for added flavour, although the spicy coating is very tasty with plain tofu.

Spicy Fried Tofu Triangles

SERVES 4

1 tbsp sea salt
4½ tsp Chinese five-spice powder
3 tbsp light brown sugar
2 garlic cloves, crushed
1 tsp grated fresh root ginger
450 g/1 lb firm tofu
vegetable oil, for deep-frying
2 leeks, shredded and halved, plus extra to garnish

1 Mix together the salt, Chinese five-spice powder, sugar, garlic and ginger in a bowl and transfer to a plate.

2 Cut the tofu cakes in half diagonally to form 2 triangles. Cut each triangle in half and then in half again to form 16 triangles.

3 Roll the tofu triangles in the spice mixture, turning to coat thoroughly. Set aside for 1 hour.

4 Heat the vegetable oil for deep-frying in a preheated wok or large, heavy-based saucepan until it is almost smoking.

5 Reduce the heat slightly, add the tofu triangles and fry for 5 minutes, until golden brown. Remove the tofu from the wok with a slotted spoon, set aside and keep warm until required.

6 Add the leeks to the wok and stir-fry for 1 minute. Remove from the wok and drain on kitchen paper.

7 Arrange the leeks on a warm serving plate and place the fried tofu on top. Garnish with the fresh shredded leek and serve immediately.

NUTRITION

Calories *224*; Sugars *17 g*; Protein *10 g*; Carbohydrate *18 g*; Fat *13 g*; Saturates *2 g*

⭐⭐⭐ moderate

🕐 1 hr 15 mins

🕐 20 mins

🍳 COOK'S TIP

Fry the tofu in batches and keep each batch warm until all of the tofu has been fried and is ready to serve.

This dish tastes as fresh as it looks. Try to get hold of baby vegetables as they look and taste so much better in this dish.

Cantonese Garden Vegetables

1 Heat the peanut oil in a preheated wok or large, heavy-based frying pan until almost smoking.

2 Add the Chinese five-spice powder, carrots, celery, leeks, mangetout, courgettes and corn cobs and stir-fry for 3–4 minutes.

3 Add the tofu to the wok and cook for a further 2 minutes, stirring gently so the tofu does not break up.

4 Stir the fresh orange juice and clear honey into the wok, reduce the heat and cook for 1–2 minutes, until slightly thickened.

5 Transfer the stir-fry to a serving dish, garnish with celery leaves and orange rind and serve with boiled rice or noodles.

SERVES 4

2 tbsp peanut oil
1 tsp Chinese five-spice powder
75 g/2¾ oz baby carrots, halved
2 celery sticks, sliced
2 baby leeks, sliced
50 g/1¾ oz mangetout
4 baby courgettes, halved lengthways
8 baby corn cobs
225 g/8 oz firm marinated tofu, cubed
4 tbsp fresh orange juice
1 tbsp clear honey
rice or noodles, to serve

to garnish
celery leaves
finely grated orange rind

NUTRITION
Calories *130*; Sugars *8 g*; Protein *6 g*;
Carbohydrate *8 g*; Fat *8 g*; Saturates *1 g*

⭐⭐ easy
🕐 5 mins
🕐 10 mins

 COOK'S TIP

Lemon juice is just as delicious as the orange juice in this stir-fry. Use 3 tablespoons of lemon juice instead of 4 tablespoons.

Rice *and* Noodles

Rice and noodles are staples in the Far East, as they are cheap, plentiful, nutritious, and delicious. They are extremely versatile ingredients and are therefore always served as part of a meal. Many rice and noodle dishes are served as accompaniments and others as main dishes combined with meat, vegetables, and fish, all flavored with fragrant spices and seasonings.

Plain rice is served to punctuate a large meal and help settle the stomach between rich, spicy courses. Noodles vary from country to country and are eaten in various forms. Thin egg noodles are made from wheat flour, water, and egg and are probably the most common in the Western diet. Available fresh or dried, they require very little cooking and are perfect for quick and easy meals.

This rice dish is made really colourful with the addition of sweetcorn and red kidney beans. It may be served as a main vegetarian dish or as a side dish.

Fried Rice *with* Spicy Beans

SERVES 4

3 tbsp sunflower oil

1 onion, finely chopped

225 g/8 oz long-grain white rice

1 green pepper, deseeded and diced

1 tsp chilli powder

600 ml/1 pint boiling water

100 g/3½ oz canned sweetcorn kernels, drained

225 g/8 oz canned red kidney beans, drained and rinsed

2 tbsp chopped fresh coriander, plus extra to garnish (optional)

1 Heat the sunflower oil in a preheated wok or large, heavy-based frying pan.

2 Add the onion to the wok and stir-fry for about 2 minutes or until the onion has softened.

3 Add the long-grain rice, green pepper and chilli powder to the wok and stir-fry for 1 minute.

4 Pour the boiling water into the wok. Bring back to the boil, then reduce the heat and leave the mixture to simmer for 15 minutes, until the water has been absorbed and the rice is tender.

5 Add the sweetcorn, kidney beans and coriander to the wok and heat through, stirring occasionally.

6 Transfer to a serving bowl and serve scattered with extra coriander, if liked.

NUTRITION

Calories *374*; Sugars *6 g*; Protein *9 g*;
Carbohydrate *64 g*; Fat *9 g*; Saturates *1 g*

easy

5 mins

25 mins

🍴 **COOK'S TIP**

For extra heat, add 1 chopped fresh red chilli with the chilli powder in step 3.

This fragrant, sweet rice is delicious served with meat, vegetable or fish dishes as part of a Chinese menu.

Fragrant Coconut Rice

1 Rinse the rice thoroughly under cold running water until the water runs completely clear.

2 Drain the rice thoroughly in a sieve set over a large bowl. (This is to remove some of the starch and to prevent the grains from sticking together.)

3 Place the rice in a wok or saucepan with the water.

4 Add the salt and coconut milk to the wok and bring to the boil.

5 Cover the wok with a lid or a lid made of foil, curved into a domed shape and resting on the sides. Reduce the heat and leave to simmer for 10 minutes.

6 Remove the lid from the wok and fluff up the rice with a fork – all of the liquid should be absorbed and the rice grains should be tender. If not, add more water and continue to simmer for a few more minutes until all of the liquid has been absorbed.

7 Spoon the rice into a warm serving bowl and scatter with the flaked coconut. Serve immediately.

SERVES 4

275 g/9½ oz long-grain white rice
600 ml/1 pint water
½ tsp salt
100 ml/3½ fl oz coconut milk
25 g/1 oz flaked coconut, to garnish

NUTRITION
Calories *306*; Sugars *2 g*; Protein *5 g*;
Carbohydrate *61 g*; Fat *6 g*; Saturates *4 g*

⭐ very easy

🕐 5 mins

🕐 15 mins

🍳 **COOK'S TIP**

Coconut milk is not the liquid found inside coconuts – that is called coconut water. Coconut milk is made from the white coconut flesh soaked in water and milk and then squeezed to extract all the flavour.

In this classic Chinese dish, boiled rice is fried with peas, spring onions and egg and flavoured with soy sauce.

Egg Fried Rice

SERVES 4

150 g/5½ oz long-grain rice
3 eggs, beaten
2 tbsp vegetable oil
2 garlic cloves, crushed
4 spring onions, chopped
125 g/4½ oz cooked peas
1 tbsp light soy sauce
pinch of salt
shredded spring onion, to garnish

1 Cook the rice in a saucepan of boiling water for 10–12 minutes, until almost cooked, but not soft. Drain the rice well, rinse under cold running water and drain thoroughly again. Leave to cool.

2 Place the beaten eggs in a saucepan and cook over a gentle heat, stirring until softly scrambled.

3 Heat the vegetable oil in a preheated wok or large, heavy-based frying pan, swirling the oil around the base of the wok until it is really hot.

4 Add the garlic, spring onions and peas and stir-fry for 1–2 minutes. Stir the rice into the wok, mixing to combine.

5 Add the eggs, light soy sauce and a pinch of salt to the wok and stir to mix in the egg thoroughly.

6 Transfer the egg fried rice to serving dishes and serve garnished with the shredded spring onion.

NUTRITION
Calories *203*; Sugars *1 g*; Protein *9 g*;
Carbohydrate *19 g*; Fat *11 g*; Saturates *2 g*

 easy

10 mins

20 mins

🍲 **COOK'S TIP**

The rice is rinsed under cold water to wash out the starch and prevent the grains from sticking together during cooking.

This dish can be served as an accompaniment or as a vegetarian main meal in itself.

Vegetable Fried Rice

1 Cook the rice in a saucepan of boiling water for 10–12 minutes, until almost cooked, but not soft. Drain the rice well, rinse under cold running water and drain thoroughly again. Leave to cool.

2 Heat the peanut oil in a preheated wok or large, heavy-based frying pan. Add the garlic and Chinese five-spice and stir-fry for 30 seconds.

3 Add the green beans, green pepper and corn cobs to the wok and stir-fry for 2 minutes.

4 Stir the bamboo shoots, tomatoes, peas and rice into the mixture in the wok and stir-fry for a further 1 minute.

5 Sprinkle with sesame oil and transfer to serving dishes. Serve immediately.

SERVES 4

125 g/4½ oz long-grain white rice
3 tbsp peanut oil
2 garlic cloves, crushed
½ tsp Chinese five-spice powder
55 g/2 oz green beans
1 green pepper, deseeded and chopped
4 baby corn cobs, sliced
25 g/1 oz bamboo shoots, chopped
3 tomatoes, skinned, deseeded and chopped
55 g/2 oz cooked peas
1 tsp sesame oil

NUTRITION
Calories 175; Sugars 3 g; Protein 3 g;
Carbohydrate 20 g; Fat 10 g; Saturates 2 g

⭐⭐ easy
🕐 10 mins
🕐 20 mins

 COOK'S TIP

Use a selection of vegetables of your choice in this recipe, cutting them to a similar size in order to ensure that they cook in the same amount of time.

Spinach is used in this recipe to give the rice a wonderful green colour. Tossed with the carrot strips, it is a really appealing dish.

Green Fried Rice

SERVES 4

150 g/5½ oz long-grain white rice
2 tbsp vegetable oil
2 garlic cloves, crushed
1 tsp grated fresh root ginger
1 carrot, cut into matchsticks
1 courgette, diced
225 g/8 oz baby spinach leaves
2 tsp light soy sauce
2 tsp light brown sugar

1 Cook the rice in a saucepan of boiling water for about 15 minutes, until tender. Drain the rice well, rinse under cold running water and then drain thoroughly again. Leave to cool.

2 Heat the oil in a preheated wok or large, heavy-based frying pan.

3 Add the garlic and ginger to the wok and stir-fry for about 30 seconds.

4 Add the carrot and courgette to the mixture in the wok and stir-fry for about 2 minutes, until the vegetables have softened, but still retain their crunch.

5 Add the baby spinach leaves and stir-fry for 1 minute, until wilted.

6 Add the rice, soy sauce and brown sugar to the wok and mix together well.

7 Transfer the green-fried rice to serving dishes and serve immediately.

NUTRITION
Calories 139; Sugars 2 g; Protein 3 g;
Carbohydrate 18 g; Fat 7 g; Saturates 1 g

easy

5 mins

20 mins

COOK'S TIP

Light soy sauce, as its name suggests, has a more delicate flavour than the sweeter, dark soy sauce, which gives the food a rich, reddish colour.

This dish is a popular choice in Chinese restaurants. Ham and prawns are mixed with vegetables in a soy-flavoured rice.

Special Fried Rice

1 Cook the rice in a saucepan of boiling water for about 15 minutes, until tender. Drain the rice well, rinse under cold running water and drain thoroughly again. Leave to cool.

2 Heat 1 tablespoon of the vegetable oil in a preheated wok or large, heavy-based frying pan.

3 Add the beaten eggs and a further 1 teaspoon of oil. Tilt the wok so that the egg covers the base to make a thin omelette.

4 Cook until lightly browned on the underside, then flip the omelette over and cook on the other side for 1 minute. Remove from the wok and leave to cool.

5 Heat the remaining oil in the wok and stir-fry the garlic and ginger for 30 seconds. Add the spring onions, peas, beansprouts, ham and prawns, then stir-fry for 2 minutes.

6 Stir in the soy sauce and rice and cook for a further 2 minutes. Transfer the rice to serving dishes. Roll up the omelette, slice it very thinly and use to garnish the rice. Serve immediately.

SERVES 4

150 g/5½ oz long-grain white rice
2 tbsp vegetable oil
2 eggs, beaten
2 garlic cloves, crushed
1 tsp grated fresh root ginger
3 spring onions, sliced
75 g/2¾ oz cooked peas
150 g/5½ oz beansprouts
225 g/8 oz shredded ham
150 g/5½ oz peeled, cooked prawns
2 tbsp light soy sauce

NUTRITION
Calories 301; Sugars 1 g; Protein 26 g; Carbohydrate 21 g; Fat 13 g; Saturates 3 g

⭐⭐ easy
🕐 5 mins
🕐 25 mins

 COOK'S TIP

As this recipe contains meat and fish, it is an ideal accompaniment to simple vegetable dishes.

Canned crab meat is used in this recipe for convenience, but fresh white crab meat is a delicious alternative.

Crab Fried Rice

SERVES 4

150 g/5½ oz long-grain white rice
2 tbsp peanut oil
125 g/4½ oz canned white crab meat, drained
1 leek, sliced
150 g/5½ oz beansprouts
2 eggs, beaten
1 tbsp light soy sauce
2 tsp lime juice
1 tsp sesame oil
salt
sliced lime, to garnish

NUTRITION
Calories *225*; Sugars *1 g*; Protein *12 g*; Carbohydrate *20 g*; Fat *11 g*; Saturates *2 g*

moderate

5 mins

25 mins

1 Cook the rice in a saucepan of boiling salted water for 15 minutes. Drain the rice well, rinse under cold running water and drain thoroughly again . Leave to cool.

2 Heat the peanut oil in a preheated wok or large, heavy-based frying pan until it is really hot.

3 Add the crab meat, leek and beansprouts to the wok and stir-fry for 2–3 minutes. Remove the mixture from the wok with a slotted spoon and set aside until required.

4 Add the eggs to the wok and cook, stirring occasionally, for 2–3 minutes, until they begin to set.

5 Stir the rice and the crab meat, leek and beansprout mixture into the eggs in the wok.

6 Add the soy sauce and lime juice. Cook for 1 minute, stirring to combine, season with salt and drizzle with the sesame oil.

7 Transfer the crab fried rice to a serving dish, garnish with the sliced lime and serve immediately.

COOK'S TIP

Cooked lobster may be used instead of the crab for a really special dish.

This soup-like main course rice dish is packed with fresh seafood and is typically Thai in flavour.

Rice *with* Seafood

1 Discard any mussels with damaged shells or open ones that do not close when firmly tapped. Heat 4 tablespoons of the stock in a large saucepan. Add the mussels, cover and shake the pan until the mussels open. Remove from the heat and discard any mussels which do not open.

2 Heat the oil in a preheated wok or large, heavy-based frying pan and fry the garlic, ginger, chilli and spring onions for 30 seconds. Add the stock and bring to the boil.

3 Stir in the rice, then add the squid, fish and prawns. Lower the heat and simmer gently for 15 minutes, or until the rice is cooked. Add the fish sauce and cooked mussels.

4 Ladle into wide bowls and sprinkle with coriander, before serving.

SERVES 4

12 mussels in their shells, cleaned
2 litres/3½ pints fish stock
2 tbsp vegetable oil
1 garlic clove, crushed
1 tsp grated fresh root ginger
1 fresh red bird's-eye chilli, chopped
2 spring onions, chopped
225 g/8 oz long-grain white rice
2 small squid, cleaned and cut into rings
100 g/3½ oz firm white fish fillet, such as halibut or monkfish, cut into chunks
100 g/3½ oz peeled raw prawns
2 tbsp Thai fish sauce
3 tbsp shredded fresh coriander, to garnish

NUTRITION
Calories 370; Sugars 0 g; Protein 27 g; Carbohydrate 52 g; Fat 8 g; Saturates 1 g

⭐⭐⭐   moderate
🕐   10 mins
🕐   25 mins

👨‍🍳 **COOK'S TIP**

You could use leftover cooked rice for this dish. Just simmer the seafood gently until cooked, then stir in the rice at the end and heat thoroughly.

This is a really colourful main meal or side dish, which tastes just as good as it looks.

Chinese Chicken Rice

SERVES 4

350 g/12 oz long-grain white rice
1 tsp turmeric
2 tbsp sunflower oil
350 g/12 oz skinless, boneless chicken breasts or thighs, sliced
1 red pepper, deseeded and sliced
1 green pepper, deseeded and sliced
1 fresh green chilli, deseeded and chopped finely
1 carrot, grated roughly
150 g/5½ oz beansprouts
6 spring onions, sliced, plus extra to garnish
2 tbsp soy sauce
salt

1 Cook the rice and turmeric in a large saucepan of lightly salted water for about 10 minutes, until the grains of rice are just tender. Drain the rice thoroughly and leave to cool.

2 Heat the sunflower oil in a preheated wok or large, heavy-based frying pan.

3 Add the chicken to the wok and stir-fry over a high heat until the chicken just begins to turn a golden colour.

4 Add the red and green peppers and green chilli to the wok and stir-fry for 2–3 minutes.

5 Add the cooked rice to the wok, a little at a time, tossing well after each addition until well combined and the grains of rice are separated.

6 Add the carrot, beansprouts and spring onions to the wok and stir-fry for a further 2 minutes.

7 Drizzle the soy sauce over the rice and toss to combine.

8 Transfer the rice to a warm serving dish, garnish with extra spring onions and serve at once.

NUTRITION
Calories 324; Sugars 4 g; Protein 24 g;
Carbohydrate 37 g; Fat 10 g; Saturates 2 g

⭐⭐⭐ moderate
🕐 10 mins
🕐 25 mins

This is a wholesome combination of rice, chicken and vegetables in a soy and ginger flavoured liquor.

Chicken *and* Rice Casserole

1 Cook the rice in a saucepan of boiling water for about 15 minutes. Drain the rice well, rinse under cold running water, then drain again thoroughly. Leave to cool.

2 Mix together the sherry, soy sauces, sugar, salt and sesame oil.

3 Stir the chicken into the soy mixture, turning to coat the chicken. Leave to marinate in the refrigerator for about 30 minutes.

4 Bring the stock to the boil in a preheated wok or large, heavy-based saucepan. Add the chicken with the marinade, mushrooms, water chestnuts, broccoli, yellow pepper and ginger.

5 Stir in the rice, reduce the heat, cover and cook for 25–30 minutes, until the chicken and vegetables are cooked through. Transfer to serving plates, garnish with chives and serve.

SERVES 4

150 g/5½ oz long-grain white rice
1 tbsp dry sherry
2 tbsp light soy sauce
2 tbsp dark soy sauce
2 tsp dark brown sugar
1 tsp salt
1 tsp sesame oil
900 g/2 lb skinless, boneless chicken meat, diced
850 ml/1½ pints chicken stock
2 open-cap mushrooms, sliced
55 g/2 oz water chestnuts, halved
75 g/2¾ oz broccoli florets
1 yellow pepper, deseeded and sliced
4 tsp grated fresh root ginger
whole chives, to garnish

NUTRITION
Calories *502*; Sugars *2 g*; Protein *55 g*; Carbohydrate *52 g*; Fat *9 g*; Saturates *3 g*

★★★   moderate
◐   35 mins
🕐   50 mins

👨‍🍳 **COOK'S TIP**

This dish works equally well with beef or pork. Chinese dried mushrooms may be used instead of the open-cap mushrooms; rehydrate in hot water before adding to the dish.

This classic dish requires little introduction as it is already a favourite amongst most Chinese food enthusiasts.

Chicken Chow Mein

SERVES 4

250 g/9 oz medium egg noodles
2 tbsp sunflower oil
275 g/9½ oz cooked chicken
  breasts, shredded
1 garlic clove, chopped finely
1 red pepper, deseeded and thinly sliced
100 g/3½ oz shiitake mushrooms, sliced
6 spring onions, sliced
100 g/3½ oz beansprouts
3 tbsp soy sauce
1 tbsp sesame oil

1 Place the egg noodles in a large bowl or dish and break them up slightly. Pour enough boiling water over the noodles to cover and leave to stand.

2 Heat the sunflower oil in a preheated wok or large, heavy-based frying pan. Add the chicken, garlic, red pepper, mushrooms, spring onions and beansprouts to the wok and stir-fry for about 5 minutes.

3 Drain the noodles thoroughly. Add the noodles to the wok, toss well and stir-fry for a further 5 minutes.

4 Drizzle the soy sauce and sesame oil over the noodle mixture in the wok and toss well until combined.

5 Transfer the noodles to warm serving bowls and serve immediately.

NUTRITION
Calories 230; Sugars 2 g; Protein 19 g;
Carbohydrate 14 g; Fat 11 g; Saturates 2 g

easy

5 mins

20 mins

🍳 **COOK'S TIP**

You can make the chow mein with a selection of vegetables instead of the chicken for a vegetarian dish, if preferred.

This is a variation of egg fried rice, which may be served as a partner to a main meal dish.

Sweet Chilli Pork Fried Rice

1 Heat the sunflower oil in a preheated wok or large, heavy-based frying pan.

2 Add the pork to the wok and stir-fry for 5 minutes.

3 Add the chilli sauce to the wok and allow to bubble, stirring, for 2–3 minutes, or until it becomes syrupy.

4 Add the onion, carrots, courgettes and bamboo shoots to the wok and stir-fry for a further 3 minutes.

5 Add the cooked rice and stir-fry for 2–3 minutes, or until the rice is completely heated through.

6 Drizzle the beaten egg over the top of the fried rice and cook, tossing the ingredients in the wok with two spoons, until the egg sets.

7 Garnish with chopped fresh parsley and serve hot with sweet chilli sauce.

SERVES 4

2 tbsp sunflower oil
450 g/1 lb pork fillet, cut into thin slices
2 tbsp sweet chilli sauce, plus extra to serve
1 onion, sliced
175 g/6 oz carrots, cut into matchsticks
175 g/6 oz courgettes, cut into matchsticks
100 g/3½ oz canned bamboo shoots, drained
275 g/9½ oz cooked long-grain white rice
1 egg, beaten
1 tbsp chopped fresh parsley, to garnish

NUTRITION
Calories *140*; Sugars *3 g*; Protein *3 g*; Carbohydrate *20 g*; Fat *17 g*; Saturates *1 g*

⊗⊗⊗   moderate

🕐   15 mins

🕐   20 mins

🍳 **COOK'S TIP**

For a really quick dish, add frozen mixed vegetables to the rice instead of the freshly prepared ones.

This quick dish uses pre-cooked rice. It is therefore ideal when time is short or for a speedy lunch-time dish.

Stir-fried Rice *with* Sausage

SERVES 4

2 tbsp sunflower oil
350 g/12 oz Chinese sausage, sliced thinly
2 tbsp soy sauce
1 onion, sliced
175 g/6 oz carrots, cut into matchsticks
175 g/6 oz frozen peas
100 g/3½ oz canned pineapple
    cubes, drained
275 g/9½ oz cooked long-grain white rice
1 egg, beaten
1 tbsp chopped fresh parsley

1 Heat the sunflower oil in a preheated wok or large, heavy-based frying pan. Add the sausage to the wok and stir-fry for 5 minutes.

2 Stir in the soy sauce and allow to bubble for about 2–3 minutes, or until it becomes syrupy.

3 Add the onion, carrots, peas and pineapple to the wok and stir-fry for a further 3 minutes.

4 Add the cooked rice to the wok and stir-fry the mixture for about 2–3 minutes, or until the rice is completely heated through.

5 Drizzle the beaten egg over the top of the rice and cook, tossing the ingredients in the wok, until the egg sets.

6 Transfer the stir-fried rice to a large, warm serving bowl and sprinkle with the fresh parsley. Serve immediately.

NUTRITION

Calories *383*; Sugars *9 g*; Protein *19 g*;
Carbohydrate *42 g*; Fat *17 g*; Saturates *4 g*

moderate

5 mins

20 mins

🖐 COOK'S TIP

Cook extra rice and freeze for later use in other rice dishes included in this book. Be sure to cool any leftover cooked rice quickly before freezing to avoid any risk of food poisoning. Reheat thoroughly before serving.

Risotto is a creamy Italian dish made with risotto rice. This Chinese version is simply delicious!

Chinese Risotto

1 Heat the groundnut oil in a preheated wok or large, heavy-based frying pan.

2 Add the onion, garlic and Chinese five-spice powder to the wok and stir-fry for 1 minute.

3 Add the Chinese sausage, carrots, green pepper and risotto rice to the wok and cook for 1 minute.

4 Gradually add the vegetable stock, a little at a time, stirring constantly until the liquid has been completely absorbed and the rice grains are tender.

5 Transfer the Chinese risotto to warm serving bowls, sprinkle with the chives and serve immediately.

SERVES 4

2 tbsp groundnut oil
1 onion, sliced
2 garlic cloves, crushed
1 tsp Chinese five-spice powder
225 g/8 oz Chinese sausage, sliced
225 g/8 oz carrots, diced
1 green pepper, deseeded and diced
275 g/9½ oz risotto rice
850 ml/1½ pints vegetable or chicken stock
1 tbsp snipped fresh chives

NUTRITION
Calories 436; Sugars 7 g; Protein 13 g; Carbohydrate 70 g; Fat 14 g; Saturates 4 g

⭐⭐   easy
🕐   5 mins
🕐   30 mins

🧑‍🍳 **COOK'S TIP**

Chinese sausage is highly flavoured and is made from chopped pork fat, pork meat and spices. Use a spicy Portuguese sausage if the Chinese sausage is unavailable.

This is a version of a favourite Thai dish, *'mee krob'*, one of those exciting dishes which can vary from one day to the next.

Crispy Rice Noodles

SERVES 4

vegetable oil for deep frying, plus 1½ tbsp
   for shallow frying
200 g/7 oz dried rice vermicelli noodles
1 onion, chopped finely
4 garlic cloves, chopped finely
1 skinless, boneless chicken breast,
   chopped finely
2 fresh red bird's-eye chillies, deseeded
   and sliced
4 tbsp dried black mushrooms, soaked and
   sliced thinly
3 tbsp dried prawns
4 spring onions, sliced
3 tbsp lime juice
2 tbsp each of soy sauce and Thai fish sauce
2 tbsp rice wine vinegar
2 tbsp soft light brown sugar
2 eggs, beaten
3 tbsp chopped fresh coriander
spring onion curls, to garnish

NUTRITION
Calories *490*; Sugars *11 g*; Protein *24 g*;
Carbohydrate *63 g*; Fat *16 g*; Saturates *2 g*

✪✪✪ moderate
🕐 10 mins
🕐 15 mins

1 Heat the oil for deep-frying in a wok or large, heavy-based frying pan until very hot. Deep-fry the noodles quickly, occasionally turning them, until puffed up, crisp and pale golden brown. Lift on to paper towels using a slotted spoon and drain well. Discard the oil.

2 Heat 1 tablespoon of the oil for shallow frying and fry the onion and garlic for 1 minute. Add the chicken and stir-fry for 3 minutes. Add the chillies, mushrooms, dried prawns and spring onions and stir-fry for 3 minutes.

3 Mix together the lime juice, soy sauce, fish sauce, rice wine vinegar and light brown sugar, then stir the mixture into the wok and cook for a further minute. Remove the wok from the heat.

4 Heat the remaining oil in a frying pan and pour in the eggs, coating the base of the pan evenly to make a thin omelette. Cook until set and golden, then turn it over and cook the other side. Turn out and roll up, then slice into long ribbon strips.

5 Toss together the fried noodles, stir-fried ingredients, coriander and omelette strips. Garnish with spring onion curls and serve at once.

These noodles are highly spiced with chilli and flavoured with sesame seeds for a nutty taste, – a true delight.

Spicy Japanese Noodles

1 Bring a large saucepan of water to the boil. Add the Japanese noodles to the pan and cook for 2–3 minutes. Drain the noodles thoroughly.

2 Toss the noodles with the sesame oil and sesame seeds.

3 Heat the sunflower oil in a preheated wok or large, heavy-based frying pan.

4 Add the onion, mangetout, carrots and cabbage to the wok and stir-fry for about 5 minutes.

5 Add the sweet chilli sauce to the wok and cook, stirring occasionally, for a further 2 minutes.

6 Add the sesame noodles to the wok, toss well to combine and heat through for a further 2–3 minutes. (You may wish to serve the noodles separately, if so transfer them to serving bowls.)

7 Transfer the mixture to warm serving bowls and garnish with the spring onions. Serve immediately.

SERVES 4

450 g/1 lb fresh Japanese noodles or dried thin egg noodles
1 tbsp sesame oil
1 tbsp sesame seeds
1 tbsp sunflower oil
1 red onion, sliced
100 g/3½ oz mangetout
175 g/6 oz carrots, sliced thinly
350 g/12 oz white cabbage, shredded
3 tbsp sweet chilli sauce
2 spring onions, sliced diagonally, to garnish

NUTRITION
Calories 381; Sugars 12 g; Protein 11 g; Carbohydrate 59 g; Fat 13 g; Saturates 2 g

★★★ moderate
🕐 5 mins
🕐 15 mins

 COOK'S TIP

If fresh Japanese noodles are difficult to find, use dried rice noodles or thin egg noodles instead.

These rice noodles and vegetables are tossed in a crunchy peanut and chilli sauce for a quick satay-flavoured recipe.

Rice Noodles *with* Beans

SERVES 4

275 g/10 oz dried flat rice noodles
3 tbsp groundnut oil
2 garlic cloves, crushed
2 shallots, sliced
225 g/8 oz green beans, sliced
100 g/3½ oz cherry tomatoes, halved
1 tsp dried chilli flakes
4 tbsp crunchy peanut butter
150 ml/5 fl oz coconut milk
1 tbsp tomato purée
sliced spring onions, to garnish

1 Place the rice noodles in a large bowl and pour over enough boiling water to cover. Leave to stand for 10 minutes.

2 Heat the groundnut oil in a preheated wok or large, heavy-based frying pan. Add the garlic and shallots and stir-fry for 1 minute.

3 Drain the rice noodles thoroughly.

4 Add the green beans and drained noodles to the wok and stir-fry for a further 5 minutes.

5 Add the cherry tomatoes to the wok and mix well.

6 Mix together the chilli flakes, peanut butter, coconut milk and tomato purée.

7 Pour the chilli, coconut mixture over the noodles, toss well to combine and heat through.

8 Transfer to warm serving dishes and garnish with the spring onions and serve immediately.

NUTRITION
Calories *259*; Sugars *9 g*; Protein *28 g*; Carbohydrate *20 g*; Fat *8 g*; Saturates 1g

   easy

🕐   5 mins

🕐   10 mins

🍽 COOK'S TIP

Add slices of chicken or beef to the recipe and stir-fry with the beans and noodles in step 4 for a more substantial main meal.

This simple, fast-food dish is sold from street food stalls in Thailand, with many varied additions of meat and vegetables.

Hot *and* Sour Noodles

1 Cook the noodles in a large pan of boiling water for 3–4 minutes, or according to the packet directions. Drain well, return to the pan, and toss with the sesame oil, then set aside.

2 Heat the chilli oil in a preheated wok or large, heavy-based frying pan and stir-fry the garlic, spring onions and button mushrooms until softened.

3 Add the black mushrooms, lime juice, soy sauce and sugar and bring to the boil. Add the noodles and toss to mix.

4 Serve spooned over the Chinese leaves, garnished with the fresh coriander and peanuts.

SERVES 4

250 g/9 oz dried medium egg noodles
1 tbsp sesame oil
1 tbsp chilli oil
1 garlic clove, crushed
2 spring onions, chopped finely
55 g/2 oz button mushrooms, sliced
40 g/1½ oz dried Chinese black mushrooms, soaked, drained and sliced
2 tbsp lime juice
3 tbsp light soy sauce
1 tsp sugar
shredded Chinese leaves, to serve

to garnish
2 tbsp shredded fresh coriander
2 tbsp chopped, toasted peanuts

NUTRITION
Calories *140*; Sugars *3 g*; Protein *3 g*;
Carbohydrate *20 g*; Fat *17 g*; Saturates *1 g*

⬤⬤⬤ moderate
🕑 15 mins
🕑 20 mins

 COOK'S TIP

Thai chilli oil is very hot, so if you want a milder flavour, use vegetable oil for the initial cooking instead, then add a dribble of chilli oil.

In this recipe, noodles are first boiled and then deep-fried for a crisp texture, then served with stir-fried vegetables.

Fried Vegetable Noodles

SERVES 4

350 g/12 oz dried thin egg noodles
2 tbsp peanut oil
2 garlic cloves, crushed
½ tsp ground star anise
1 carrot, cut into matchsticks
1 green pepper, deseeded and cut into matchsticks
1 onion, quartered and sliced
125 g/4½ oz broccoli florets
75 g/2¾ oz bamboo shoots
1 celery stick, sliced
1 tbsp light soy sauce
150 ml/5 fl oz vegetable stock
oil, for deep-frying
1 tsp cornflour
2 tsp water

NUTRITION
Calories 229; Sugars 4 g; Protein 5 g;
Carbohydrate 20 g; Fat 15 g; Saturates 2 g

moderate

5 mins

25 mins

1 Cook the noodles in a saucepan of boiling water for 1–2 minutes. Drain well and rinse under cold running water. Leave the noodles to drain thoroughly in a colander until required.

2 Heat the peanut oil in a preheated wok or large, heavy-based frying pan until smoking. Reduce the heat, then add the garlic and ground star anise and stir-fry for 30 seconds. Add the remaining vegetables and stir-fry for 1–2 minutes.

3 Add the soy sauce and vegetable stock to the wok and cook over a low heat for 5 minutes.

4 Heat the oil for deep-frying in a separate wok or saucepan to 180°C/350°F, or until a cube of bread browns in 30 seconds.

5 Using a fork, twist the drained noodles and form them into 4 rounds. Deep-fry them in batches until crisp, turning once. Leave the noodles to drain on kitchen paper.

6 Blend the cornflour with the water to form a paste and stir into the vegetables. Bring to the boil, stirring until the sauce is thickened and clear.

7 Arrange the noodles on warm serving plates, spoon the vegetables on top and serve immediately.

Fruit combines well with the sweet peppers, chilli and peanut dressing in this delicious warm salad.

Noodle *and* Mango Salad

1 Cook the noodles in a saucepan of boiling water following the packet directions until tender, then drain well.

2 Heat the groundnut oil in a preheated wok or large, heavy-based frying pan.

3 Add the shallots, garlic, chilli and red and green pepper to the wok and stir-fry for 2–3 minutes.

4 Drain the egg noodles thoroughly in a colander. Add the drained noodles and mango to the wok and heat through for about 2 minutes.

5 Transfer the noodle and mango salad to warm serving dishes and scatter with chopped peanuts.

6 To make the dressing, mix together the peanut butter, coconut milk and tomato purée, then spoon it over the noodle salad. Serve immediately.

SERVES 4

250 g/9 oz dried medium egg noodles
2 tbsp groundnut oil
4 shallots, sliced
2 garlic cloves, crushed
1 fresh red chilli, deseeded and sliced
1 red pepper, deseeded and sliced
1 green pepper, deseeded and sliced
1 ripe mango, peeled, stoned and sliced into thin strips
25 g/1 oz salted peanuts, chopped

dressing
4 tbsp peanut butter
100 ml/3½ fl oz coconut milk
1 tbsp tomato purée

NUTRITION

Calories *368*; Sugars *11 g*; Protein *11 g*; Carbohydrate *24 g*; Fat *26 g*; Saturates *5 g*

⭐⭐ easy
🕐 15 mins
🕐 15 mins

🍳 COOK'S TIP

If preferred, gently heat the peanut dressing before pouring it over the warm noodle salad.

Cellophane or thread noodles can be easily re-heated, unlike other noodles which must be served as soon as they are cooked.

Yellow Bean Noodles

SERVES 4

175 g/6 oz cellophane noodles
1 tbsp peanut oil
1 leek, sliced
2 garlic cloves, crushed
450 g/1 lb minced chicken
425 ml/15 fl oz chicken stock
1 tsp chilli sauce
2 tbsp yellow bean sauce
4 tbsp light soy sauce
1 tsp sesame oil
chopped fresh chives, to garnish

1 Place the cellophane noodles in a bowl, pour enough boiling water over to cover and soak for 15 minutes.

2 Drain the noodles thoroughly and cut into short lengths with a pair of kitchen scissors.

3 Heat the oil in a preheated wok or large, heavy-based frying pan and stir-fry the leek and garlic for 30 seconds.

4 Add the chicken to the wok and stir-fry for 4–5 minutes, until it is completely cooked through.

5 Add the chicken stock, chilli sauce, yellow bean sauce and soy sauce to the wok and cook for 3–4 minutes.

6 Add the drained noodles and sesame oil to the wok and cook, tossing to mix well, for 4–5 minutes.

7 Spoon the mixture into warm serving bowls, sprinkle with chopped chives and serve immediately.

NUTRITION

Calories 212; Sugars 0.5 g; Protein 28 g;
Carbohydrate 10 g; Fat 7 g; Saturates 2 g

easy

5 mins

30 mins

COOK'S TIP

Cellophane noodles are readily available from most supermarkets and Chinese supermarkets.

Fish and fruit are tossed with a trio of peppers in this spicy dish, which can be served with noodles for a quick, healthy meal.

Noodles *with* Cod *and* Mango

1 Place the egg noodles in a large bowl and pour enough boiling water over to cover. Leave to stand for about 10 minutes.

2 Place the cod in a large bowl. Add the paprika and toss well to coat the fish.

3 Heat the sunflower oil in a preheated wok or large, heavy-based frying pan.

4 Add the onion, orange, red and green peppers and baby corn cobs to the wok and stir-fry for about 5 minutes.

5 Add the cod to the wok together with the sliced mango and stir-fry for a further 2–3 minutes, or until the fish is tender.

6 Add the beansprouts to the wok and toss well to combine.

7 Mix together the tomato ketchup, soy sauce, sherry and cornflour. Add the mixture to the wok and cook, stirring occasionally, until the juices thicken.

8 Drain the noodles thoroughly and transfer to warm serving bowls. Transfer the cod and mango stir-fry to separate serving bowls.

SERVES 4

250 g/9 oz dried egg noodles
450 g/1 lb skinless cod fillet, cut into thin strips
1 tbsp paprika
2 tbsp sunflower oil
1 red onion, sliced
1 orange pepper, deseeded and sliced
1 red pepper, deseeded and sliced
1 green pepper, deseeded and sliced
100 g/3½ oz baby corn cobs, lengthways halved
1 mango, peeled, stoned and sliced
100 g/3½ oz beansprouts
2 tbsp tomato ketchup
2 tbsp soy sauce
2 tbsp medium sherry
1 tsp cornflour

NUTRITION
Calories *274*; Sugars *11 g*; Protein *25 g*; Carbohydrate *26 g*; Fat *8 g*; Saturates *1 g*

✪✪✪   moderate

🕐   10 mins

🕐   25 mins

This dish combines meat, vegetables, prawns and noodles in a curried coconut sauce. Serve as a main meal or as an accompanying dish.

Special Noodles

SERVES 4

250 g/9 oz dried thin rice noodles
4 tbsp groundnut oil
2 garlic cloves, crushed
2 fresh red chillies, deseeded and
   very chopped finely
1 tsp grated fresh root ginger
2 tbsp Madras curry paste
2 tbsp rice wine vinegar
1 tbsp caster sugar
225 g/8 oz cooked ham, shredded finely
100 g/3½ oz canned water chestnuts,
   drained and sliced
100 g/3½ oz mushrooms, sliced
100 g/3½ oz frozen peas
1 red pepper, seeded and sliced thinly
100 g/3½ oz cooked peeled prawns
2 large eggs
4 tbsp coconut milk
25 g/1 oz desiccated coconut
2 tbsp chopped fresh coriander, to garnish

NUTRITION
Calories *409*; Sugars *12 g*; Protein *24 g*;
Carbohydrate *28 g*; Fat *23 g*; Saturates *8 g*

⭐⭐⭐   moderate
🕐   5 mins
🕐   25 mins

1 Place the rice noodles in a large bowl, pour enough boiling water over to cover and leave to soak for about 10 minutes. Drain the noodles thoroughly, then toss with 2 tablespoons of the groundnut oil.

2 Heat the remaining groundnut oil in a preheated wok or large, heavy-based frying pan until the oil is very hot.

3 Add the garlic, chillies, ginger, curry paste, rice wine vinegar and caster sugar to the wok and stir-fry for 1 minute.

4 Add the ham, water chestnuts, mushrooms, peas and red pepper to the wok and stir-fry for 5 minutes.

5 Add the noodles and prawns to the wok and stir-fry for 2 minutes.

6 In a small bowl, beat together the eggs and coconut milk. Drizzle over the mixture in the wok and stir-fry until the egg sets.

7 Add the desiccated coconut and fresh coriander to the wok and toss to combine. Transfer the noodles to warm serving dishes and serve.

These noodles could make a meal in themselves. Although if served as an accompaniment, they are ideal with plain vegetable or fish dishes.

Curried Prawn Noodles

1 Cook the noodles in a pan of boiling water for 3–4 minutes. Drain the noodles well, rinse under cold water and drain again.

2 Heat 2 tablespoons of the oil in a wok. Add the onion and ham and stir-fry for 1 minute. Add the curry powder and stir-fry for a further 30 seconds.

3 Stir the noodles and fish stock into the wok and cook for 2–3 minutes. Remove the noodles from the wok and keep warm.

4 Heat the remaining oil in the wok. Add the prawns, garlic and spring onions and stir-fry for about 1 minute.

5 Stir in the remaining ingredients. Pour the mixture over the noodles, toss well and garnish with fresh chives to serve.

SERVES 4

225 g/8 oz dried egg noodles
4 tbsp vegetable oil
1 onion, sliced
2 ham slices, shredded
2 tbsp Chinese curry powder
150 ml/5 fl oz fish stock
225 g/8 oz peeled, raw prawns
2 garlic cloves, crushed
6 spring onions, chopped
1 tbsp light soy sauce
2 tbsp hoisin sauce
1 tbsp dry sherry
2 tsp lime juice
snipped fresh chives, to garnish

NUTRITION
Calories *246*; Sugars *1 g*; Protein *17 g*;
Carbohydrate *14 g*; Fat *14 g*; Saturates *2 g*

⭐⭐ easy
🕐 5 mins
🕐 15 mins

🅦 **COOK'S TIP**

Hoisin sauce is made from soya beans, sugar, flour, vinegar, salt, garlic, chilli and sesame oil. Sold in cans or jars, it will keep in the refrigerator for several months once opened if kept in a sealed container.

Delicately scented with sesame, lime and coriander, these noodles make an unusual lunch or supper dish.

Sesame Noodles *with* Prawns

SERVES 4

1 garlic clove, chopped
1 spring onion, chopped
1 small fresh red chilli, deseeded and sliced
1 tbsp chopped, fresh coriander
300 g/10½ oz dried fine egg noodles
2 tbsp vegetable oil
2 tsp sesame oil
1 tsp shrimp paste
225 g/8 oz peeled raw prawns
2 tbsp lime juice
2 tbsp Thai fish sauce
1 tsp sesame seeds, toasted

1 Place the garlic, onion, chilli and coriander in a pestle and mortar and grind to a smooth paste.

2 Cook the noodles in a saucepan of boiling water for 4 minutes, or according to the packet directions.

3 Meanwhile, heat the oils in a preheated wok or large, heavy-based frying pan. Stir in the shrimp paste and ground coriander paste. Stir over a medium heat for 1 minute.

4 Add the prawns and stir-fry for 2 minutes. Stir in the lime juice and fish sauce and cook for a further 1 minute.

5 Drain the noodles and add them to the wok, tossing well. Sprinkle with the sesame seeds and serve.

NUTRITION
Calories *430*; Sugars *2 g*; Protein *23 g*;
Carbohydrate *56 g*; Fat *15 g*; Saturates *3 g*

easy

5 mins

10 mins

COOK'S TIP

The roots of coriander are widely used in Thai cooking, so if you can buy fresh coriander with the root attached, the whole plant can be used in this dish for maximum flavour. If not, just use the stems and leaves.

This is a special and well-known dish, which is a delicious meal in itself, packed with chicken, prawns and vegetables.

Singapore Noodles

1 Place the noodles in a large bowl and pour enough boiling water over to cover. Leave to stand for 4 minutes, or until soft, then drain well.

2 Heat 2 tablespoons of the oil in a preheated wok or large, heavy-based frying pan. Add the eggs and stir until set. Remove the cooked eggs from the wok, set aside and keep warm.

3 Add the remaining oil to the wok. Add the garlic and chilli powder and stir-fry for 30 seconds.

4 Add the chicken and stir-fry for 4–5 minutes, until just beginning to brown.

5 Stir in the celery, green pepper, spring onions, water chestnuts and chillies and cook for a further 8 minutes, or until the chicken is cooked through.

6 Add the prawns and the drained noodles to the wok, together with the beansprouts, and toss to mix well.

7 Break the cooked egg with a fork and arrange it over the noodles, then drizzle over the sesame oil. Serve immediately.

SERVES 4

225 g/8 oz dried egg noodles
6 tbsp vegetable oil
4 eggs, beaten
3 garlic cloves, crushed
1½ tsp chilli powder
225 g/8 oz skinless, boneless chicken, cut into thin strips
3 celery sticks, sliced
1 green pepper, deseeded and sliced
4 spring onions, sliced
25 g/1 oz water chestnuts, quartered
2 fresh red chillies, sliced
300 g/10 oz peeled, cooked prawns
175 g/6 oz beansprouts
2 tsp sesame oil

NUTRITION
Calories *627*; Sugars *3 g*; Protein *44 g*;
Carbohydrate *44 g*; Fat *32 g*; Saturates *4 g*

⭐⭐⭐ moderate

🕐 5 mins

🕐 20 mins

 COOK'S TIP

When mixing pre-cooked ingredients into the dish, such as the egg and noodles, ensure that they are heated right through when ready to serve.

The combination of ingredients in this classic Thai noodle dish varies, but it commonly contains a mixture of pork and prawns or other seafood.

Pad Thai Noodles

SERVES 4

250 g/9 oz dried rice stick noodles
3 tbsp groundnut oil
3 garlic cloves, chopped finely
125 g/4½ oz pork fillet, chopped into
   5-mm/¼-inch pieces
200 g/7 oz peeled cooked prawns
1 tbsp caster sugar
3 tbsp Thai fish sauce
1 tbsp tomato ketchup
1 tbsp lime juice
2 eggs, beaten
125 g/4½ oz beansprouts

to garnish
1 tsp dried red chilli flakes
2 spring onions, sliced thickly
2 tbsp chopped fresh coriander

1 Place the rice noodles in a large bowl and pour enough boiling water over to cover. Leave to stand for 10 minutes, or according to the packet instructions. Drain well and set aside.

2 Heat the oil in a preheated wok or large, heavy-based frying pan and fry the garlic over a high heat for 30 seconds. Add the pork and stir-fry for 2–3 minutes until browned.

3 Stir in the prawns, then add the sugar, fish sauce, tomato ketchup and lime juice, and continue to stir-fry for a further 30 seconds.

4 Stir in the eggs and stir-fry until lightly set. Stir in the noodles, then add the beansprouts and stir-fry for a further 30 seconds to cook lightly.

5 Turn out on to a serving dish and scatter with chilli flakes, spring onions and coriander to garnish.

NUTRITION
Calories *477*; Sugars *6 g*; Protein *26 g*;
Carbohydrate *60 g*; Fat *14 g*; Saturates *3 g*

⭐⭐   easy
🕐   10 mins
🕐   15 mins

 COOK'S TIP

Drain the rice noodles well before adding to the pan, as excess moisture will spoil the texture of the dish.

This dish is usually served as a snack or light meal, yet, it also makes a delicious accompaniment to plain vegetable, meat and fish dishes.

Cantonese Fried Noodles

1 Cook the noodles in a saucepan of boiling water for 2–3 minutes. Drain well, rinse under cold running water and drain thoroughly again.

2 Heat 1 tablespoon of the oil in a preheated wok or large, heavy-based frying pan, swirling it around until it is very hot

3 Add the noodles and stir-fry for 1–2 minutes. Drain the noodles and set aside until required.

4 Heat the remaining oil in the wok. Add the beef and stir-fry for 2–3 minutes. Add the cabbage, bamboo shoots, spring onions and beans to the wok and stir-fry for 1–2 minutes.

5 Add the soy sauce, beef stock, dry sherry and light brown sugar to the wok, stirring to mix well.

6 Stir the noodles into the mixture in the wok, tossing to mix well. Transfer to serving bowls, garnish with chopped parsley and serve immediately.

SERVES 4

350 g/12 oz dried medium egg noodles
3 tbsp vegetable oil
675 g/1½ lb lean beef steak, cut into thin strips
125 g/4½ oz green cabbage, shredded
75 g/2¾ oz bamboo shoots
6 spring onions, sliced
25 g/1 oz green beans, halved
1 tbsp dark soy sauce
2 tbsp beef stock
1 tbsp dry sherry
1 tbsp light brown sugar
2 tbsp chopped fresh parsley, to garnish

NUTRITION
Calories *385*; Sugars *6 g*; Protein *38 g*; Carbohydrate *21 g*; Fat *17 g*; Saturates *4 g*

⭐⭐   easy

        5 mins

        15 mins

Index